The Family

The Family

UNCHANGING

PRINCIPLES FOR

CHANGING

TIMES

DOROTHY KELLEY PATTERSON

Foreword by Dr. Laura Schlessinger

PUBLISHING GROUP

Nashville, Tennessee

© 2002
by Dorothy Kelley Patterson
All rights reserved
Printed in the United States of America
978–0–8054–2151–4

Published by B&H Publishing Group,
Nashville, Tennessee

Dewey Decimal Classification: 248
Subject Heading: FAMILY

Scripture text is quoted from the New King James Version,
copyright © 1979, 1980, 1982, Thomas Nelson, Inc., Publishers.

Library of Congress Cataloging-in-Publication Data

Patterson, Dorothy Kelley, 1943–
  The family : unchanging principles for changing times / Dorothy
  Kelley Patterson.
    p. cm.
  Includes bibliographical references.
  ISBN 0–8054–2151–3 (pb.)
  1. Family—Religious life. 2. Family—Religious aspects—
  Christianity. I. Title.

BV4526.2 .P38 2002
248.4—dc21
                                                    2001037946
          2 3 4 5 7 8 9 10   13 12 11 10 09

TO PARENTS, THE ROCK FROM
WHICH I WAS HEWN

Charles Kelley, a man of integrity and spiritual strength, introduced me to God by his provision, protection, and leadership in my childhood home. **Doris Kelley** carefully and consistently nurtured me physically, mentally, emotionally, and spiritually. Showed me in a unique way the heart of God.

T. A. Patterson, as my first pastor, was instrumental in bringing me to Jesus and building the foundations of my faith. **Roberta ("Honey") Patterson,** mentor, friend, and counselor, began equipping me for service in the kingdom of Christ before I married her son.

TO SISTERS AND BROTHERS,
MY FOREVER FRIENDS

David and Rima Amad were grafted into our family circle. David is my soulmate from high school and Rima, a kindred spirit devoted to family and hearth.

Kathy Kelley shares a love of books and passion for opening windows to the world for children.

Russell and Charlene Kaemmerling, who lovingly care for our retired parents, are my personal angels of mercy.

Chuck and Rhonda Kelley work in ministry as do we. Chuck is strong and wise; Rhonda encourages with her optimistic spirit.

Steve and Eileen Turrentine give themselves sacrificially to serving churches in pioneer areas.

TO NIECES AND NEPHEWS,
SOURCES OF PRIDE

Yaser challenges me with his inquisitive mind and sharp wit. **Nadia** is full of laughter and makes a room sparkle.

Beth has a servant's heart and ministers to us all; **Angie** has lots of creativity and surprises us with her special creations. As a fireman, **Perry** is a committed public servant and a wonderful "fixer"; **Kelley** is a diligent worker; and **Claire** is a young journalist keeping me abreast of family news.

Sarah has a sensitive heart and continues on her spiritual pilgrimage.

And great niece Brittany **Kate** Wheeler is a bundle of love whose hugs and kisses comfort me. **Marty** Brock is a new gift of life.

TO MY HUSBAND, CHILDREN, AND GRAND-CHILDREN—MY PASSION AND LIFE'S WORK

Paige—my provider, protector, and leader—through his love has been the human force molding and fashioning me into who I am.

Armour and his wife **Rachel** lovingly encourage me to relax and enjoy the blessings of solitude.

Mark is a godly pastor and capable scholar walking in truth. **Carmen**, a living fount of joy, has committed her primary energies and creativity to her home; and that makes me happy.

Abigail Leigh and **Rebekah Elizabeth** are my joy and delight! Their hearts are already sensitive to the Lord.

Noche, the **Squealer**, and **Patmos**—the granddogs—are also part of our family circle!

Contents

Foreword

BY DR. LAURA SCHLESSINGER

IT'S VERY GRATIFYING TO ME that a significant number of books are being published supporting the cultural significance of the family and the value of the marriage commitment to the health and happiness of all family members. This is an issue I have been concerned about for years, because in my position as a radio talk show host, in talking to thousands of callers each year, I am painfully aware of their increasing confusion, selfishness, and lack of guidance from parents, mentors, or clergy. And those who pay the price are, inevitably, children. They call me, too—and break my heart, day after day.

Tragically, they are the victims of family and societal degeneration. Kids want, need, and deserve a comitted mom and dad who love them, protect them, and teach them right from wrong. When they don't have this, they grow up with increased levels of stress, depression, and anxiety as well as a lack of patience, compassion, and morality.

In this book, Dorothy Patterson explains that families have been the cornerstone on which our nation rests. She goes on, with intelligence, insight, and strong faith, to detail the moral and emotional breakdown of American families and how it is affecting our society. But she doesn't just leave readers in the problem. She shows that with a dedication to G-d,* understanding of Scripture, and commitment to marriage, you can create a strong family that functions effectively, efficiently, and with love.

I totally agree with Dr. Patterson that children and families need a strong belief in G-d* and the family practice of religion in order to strengthen the family unit and prepare children to be good citizens, responsible adults, and caring parents, themselves. No matter what problems and challenges your family may be facing, *The Family* will help you by providing a biblical roadmap to become successful in your life, in your marriage, in parenting your children, and in "doing the right thing."

*Orthodox Jews do not spell out the word God.

Preface

CHILDREN ARE A FAMILY TREASURE—not a community trust. Since the family forms the core of life, women should be more precious than jewels and children ought to be an asset. The family has been the cornerstone on which the nation is resting. Society now seems intent on disintegrating the family. Children are being passed from the control of their parents to the rule of "community experts" who are supposedly better able to prepare them for the complexities of life.

The old African proverb "It takes a whole village to raise a child" affirms that no child will be reared in isolation from the larger community and world. But families gather to make a village! They adopt common goals and projects, and the village works to protect and nurture the next generation. The physical, emotional, and spiritual security inherent in a family usually leads to satisfying and productive lives.

Some say, "It takes a church to raise a child." The church made a unique contribution to my life and to the lives of my children. My granddaughters Abigail and Rebekah love to go to "church church"! Churches are important team members for spiritual nurture that begins in the home. Yet someone has to get the child to church! Ultimately, mother and father stand accountable to God for rearing their children up into godliness.

Freedom to be yourself does not mean liberty to thumb your nose at others. Especially is this important within the family where you learn to relate to others, while making unique contributions balanced with a willingness to conform to life "in community" with others. Once you learn to interact with others in your family, you are better equipped to take your place in the "village" and the world.

God *started* civilization with a family—not a village or a religious institution. One man and one woman were created by God for the purpose of linking their lives in an exclusive, monogamous relationship with each other. The first couple was commissioned by God to have dominion over the world and to extend the generations.

This man and woman who were uniquely committed to each other formed the first family. As their descendants multiplied, families extended to clans; communities developed; nations came into being. But the founding document of civilization revered by Jews and Christians—that is, Holy Scripture—offers no evidence that the nurturing of children was primarily a community responsibility. Rather mother and father are to rear their own children unto the Lord and guide them into becoming contributing members of an ongoing society! It takes committed parents—not merely a good "village" or willing congregation—to rear a child. Families band together to establish a healthy society.

The family acts as a watchman on the wall to protect the community from alien values and untested changes. No schoolroom, government program, or system of religion is in position to lay spiritual and moral foundations for the family.

Biblical references are provided at the ends of each chapter. Many sociological and psychological principles find themselves in harmony with what God said through the authors of Scripture thousands of years ago! Often your gut instincts are in sync with the Bible—the oldest textbook available on the family. But bedrock truth remains the same!

Introduction

EVERY FAMILY BECOMES A LIVING MOSAIC. My husband and I have different family backgrounds. My mother, an orphan from childhood, was reared by her grandparents. My father worked with his six siblings to help support his family.

The Weisiger/Kelley and Turner/Patterson grandparents of Paige and me were faithful to give their children a strong faith in God and responsible work ethic. Although these families were living in poverty in comparison to many of their contemporaries, they never considered accepting, much less demanding, welfare or handouts. Each family member worked hard, lived frugally, and shared generously.

The Pattersons and Kelleys established their homes on the foundations laid by their parents, but they brought to their respective families new family traditions. My husband's parents gained education and influence in the religious arena. Paige's father served as the senior pastor of influential churches and as a prominent denominational leader in the Southern Baptist Convention, extending his influence worldwide. Paige's mother was a musician, author, artist, and gracious hostess. The Pattersons were truly citizens of the world! They added "children," including a Palestinian "son," who after accruing personal wealth and position remains an active part of our family; as well as a Japanese "daughter" and Mexican "son," who lived in the household while completing university studies. Ethnic meals, culturally diverse sibling

I

interaction, and historical vignettes with nationalistic color introduced us to the world!

My mother and father married and established their home while Dad served his country as a pilot during the war. He moved from employee to partner and finally became the owner of a prosperous business. My mother had business school training but chose to devote herself to rearing five children. They, too, were marked by a deeply rooted faith and a commitment to consistent service in their community. They made available to their children the best in education and opened the doors of their home to anyone God sent to its threshold.

In our family heritage both grandparents and parents were immersed in faith in God and committed to honor the Bible as God's Word. Our heritage was unequivocally linked to a determination that the family was the most important block in society—surpassing the government, the community, and the church. Also, our respective families believed that family responsibility included the investment of time and resources in every area of life.

My mother nurtured my siblings and me daily in the home, meeting our physical needs with nutritious meals and ministering to emotional and spiritual needs with loving encouragement. She knew our teachers and monitored what they were teaching. She was aware of our infirmities. She observed our friendships and activities. She accompanied us to church and opened our home to youth events. She was available for field trips, athletic events, and music concerts. She was always an integral part of our lives.

My father worked hard, giving us by word and lifestyle a clear work ethic. He was without doubt the provider, protector, and leader of our family. When challenging homework or overwhelming projects plagued us, he always appeared at just the right moment.

My husband's mother had some graduate education and many gifts. She exercised her creativity by writing original stories, poems, and even several books. She illustrated the stories she wrote for her grandchildren with her own artwork. She was not as involved in Paige's athletic endeavors and other extracurricular events. However, she had a heart for the world and passed to Paige an appreciation for the people of the world and a curiosity about the cultures they represented. She extended hospitality to many, and she had a committed interest in her son's ministry as a preacher.

Paige's father was a man who cast an awesome shadow. His moral ascendancy and statesmanlike demeanor gave him tremendous stature and opened doors for unusual leadership within the denomination he served. He was very involved in his work and ministry and did not have hands-on involvement in Paige's academic and extracurricular activities. However, the on-the-job training for ministry Paige received from his father could never be matched in any classroom. "Patee," as we affectionately called him, was a man of great wisdom and impeccable character.

When Paige and I married, we meshed together the wonderful heritages from our respective families. We built upon the "old" foundations, while finding new ways of fleshing out our assignment to continue the generations and exercise dominion over the world.

From my family we caught the spirit of humble, committed volunteerism, especially in the church and community. My parents were faithful supporters and participants in all the church's programs. They had limited education, extending only to their respective professional training programs, but they sacrificed to provide education for their children. They knew teachers, supervised the doing of all assignments, and encouraged extra enrichment activities. We also caught from them a spirit of tight-knit relationships within the extended family.

From my husband's family, we acquired a vision of the world and its people. We learned history by tracing its steps. We have made the necessary sacrifices to enable both our son and daughter, as well as our son-in-love, to experience first-hand the diversity among the nations, the needs of those who live in underdeveloped countries, and the lessons to be learned from other ethnic groups.

Paige and I, too, have included an international touch within our family. Alberto from Brazil and Mitsunobu from Japan lived in our household while completing university training. In addition, student interns, though not actually living in our home, entered our family circle for brief periods through the years. My husband and I have a large personal library and have passed on to our children and grandchildren a love for books and learning.

From both of our families, we have observed a commitment to service—within the family, in the church, and in the community. From both families we have observed role relationships based on the Judeo-Christian model found in the earliest extant document on the family, the Bible. From both family traditions come familial pride and the commitment to love, encourage, and care for one another.

For our extended family another generation has begun. Our daughter and son-in-love share the faith in God established in their birth families; they have had biblical marriage modeled by mothers and fathers committed to monogamous union. Mark and Carmen have continued the tradition of weaving their children into life and ministry. Carmen is keeping her home and nurturing her children, even with financial and professional sacrifices. Mark is eager to support her in that decision by providing, protecting, and leading.

Our son Armour entered his third decade still single, but now he has found his soulmate. They, too, are committed to marriage as an inviolate covenant bearing the divine imprimature. Armour uses his creativity and disciplined research in writing both fiction and nonfiction books.

Paige and I continue to fashion and mold our home as do our children. Each is and will be unique; yet all are bound by the heritage of character and traditions from those who have gone before.[1]

Producing a clear and concise definition of the family is going to be clouded by the culture and its diversity, by the historical milieu and its breadth, by the polarization between the heritage of the past and the reality of the present worldview as well as by what may come for future generations. The common dilemma of the human race in every generation seems to rest in the fact that every man and woman is drawn to do what is right in his own eyes.

The result is often confusion and misunderstanding as family members become so absorbed in looking after personal interests that each becomes more self-centered than God-centered. To be God-centered is to be family sensitive and other conscious. The desperation and tragedy that characterize modern families is not limited to a certain ethnic background, particular geographical region, select economic bracket, or common religious commitment. The problems that exist are not stereotyped to exclude or pinpoint a particular set of circumstances. The breakdown continues unabated and seemingly worldwide, and all must work together to seek solutions.

This volume does not describe an ivory-tower or utopian Camelot in which a family could flourish. Rather, its purpose is to return to basic wisdom and reflect on those characteristics that have brought success and prosperity to the family—in whatever generation and under a myriad of circumstances! You can learn what makes a family function effectively from those who have gone before as well as from people living contentedly a continent away in diverse circumstances. However, you will achieve more success and reach your goals more speedily if you look to the handbook that records the starting of the human race. In the Bible you read about the purposes of God who created the man and woman and about His design for how they are to relate to each other.[2]

1. Isa. 51:1–2.
2. Gen. 1:26–2:25.

1

If It Ain't Broken, Don't Fix It!

MORAL DECAY IS EATING AWAY the foundations of the family and reflects a nation in crisis. Living together in lieu of marriage no longer engenders shame. Widespread cohabitation before marriage is not done under cover. Adultery and fornication are practiced without guilt; legal abortion, easy divorce, and the embracing of feminism and other ideologies that attack the family are now so commonplace that they hardly raise an eyebrow. Violence in neighborhood schools, synagogues, and churches is rampant. Bold efforts to legalize and legitimize homosexuality and lesbianism are moving to the public arena. Attitudes have moved from being relationship oriented to being individual centered. Commitments, even if set in public covenant, have little long-term importance. These changes reflect a decline in the traditional Judeo-Christian morality that for centuries has characterized the best in society. The family has been dealt a devastating blow.

In Israel the Kibbutz movement showcased nonparental child care as being more efficient and profitable for community productivity. Children not only spent the day away from their parents with caretakers for education and entertainment, but they also slept and ate in a separate building. This paradigm illustrated perfectly the contrast between the "village" care of children and parental child rearing. Most modern Kibbutzim have abandoned community custodial care and returned to placing the responsibility for rearing children with parents, where it belongs! Social experimentation lost out to traditional wisdom based upon divine patterns found in Scripture.

Taxation has levied an unrealistic burden on families. American citizens entered the new millennium with a "marriage tax" that assessed married couples, especially when mothers chose the home over the marketplace, with a heavier tax burden than single-parent households or couples who choose cohabitation as a substitute for marriage. Such couples have a preferable position to married couples; that is, they are granted rights without responsibilities. Their number-one priority is personal, immediate fulfillment rather than a long-term commitment to another person.

Mothers with children in day care centers are subsidized, while mothers who care for their own children at home not only receive little economic recognition for their contribution to society but also are penalized through the tax system. The tax benefits linked to a parent's day care expenses have penalized parents for spending time with their children and rewarded parents who elect to keep their children in day care! Surely there must be a more equitable way to help all parents—like replacing these preferential provisions with a new per-child tax credit that would provide significant tax relief to all families with children.

IS THIS PROGRESS?

The self-sufficiency of the family before the nineteenth century taught children the skills and means to follow a trade, to grow their own food, to make their own clothes, and to provide their own energy and transportation. They also received moral training and learned the basic skills of reading, writing, and arithmetic in their own homes. Teachers were employed and classrooms were established only *to serve and accommodate the needs of families.*

With the nineteenth-century Industrial Revolution, people left the agrarian society and moved to cities. Families became more dependent on mass-produced goods, and the workplace was separated from the home. Buying factory-produced food and clothing became more efficient for homemakers. Schools and teachers became partners in a national education system and in so doing managed to usurp many functions once performed by parents.

Postmodernism has dawned. Many consider home more a prison than a haven. They prefer spending time with peers in the workplace to investing hours in relationships with their children. Products are more important than people. For many parents, children are an ornamental luxury or economic liability. Parental "quality" care often becomes a weekly, penciled-in, evening time slot. Children indeed do need *quality* time—but in a large *quantity!*

Schools become managers of child rearing and education. Teachers and educational administrators assume a position of dictating to parents how a child's life is to be molded, including the kind of home environment he is to have. One morning a week of child care moves to one day, extends to three mornings, continues to five days, and finally becomes daily before and after-school care so that even preschoolers have more time with an array of teachers and caregivers than with their own parents. Educators dictate health requirements, mealtime nutrition, moral standards, and in the process they demand more money to cover the cost of these new responsibilities. *The bottom line for parents is this: How can you expect people to do for money what you will not do for love!*

Infants, children, and teens need more than education and socialization from well-trained experts; they long for loving affection and an unhurried atmosphere with their own parents investing a quantity of quality time. In a YMCA survey 21 percent of twelve- to fifteen-year-olds wished their busy parents had more time to spend with them; 47 percent of the fathers and 38 percent of the mothers indicated they were trying to find more time to spend with their kids. Everyone seems to be obsessed with a "just-in-time" framework—no opportunity to smell the roses or see the people!

The massive entry of women into the workplace has not given mother and father more time for family by spreading the economic burden between them. Instead, both mother and father have been drawn away from the family. Men and women are working more and enjoying it less.

An AFL-CIO poll reveals that 46 percent of all women who are married or living with someone work a different schedule than their partners.[1] Wives in two-parent homes are marked more and more by the need to work different hours than their husbands to balance parenting responsibilities or avoid child care costs or to pursue a more appealing career. But this unnatural situation tends to add more stress to the marital situation without solving the dilemma of a family of ships passing in the night!

Parents not only have limited time with their children, but they also have less support from members of the extended family who may themselves be fragmented and far from any family ties. A woman no longer devotes herself exclusively to family, that is, nurturing and supervising children and maintaining the home, just as a man no longer devotes himself exclusively to the workplace, that is, providing the family's needed food and shelter. The bottom line is that no one is charged with rearing the children and keeping the home. Everyone's responsibility is done by no one!

During the Persian Gulf War, mothers in the military left nursing infants to go to a war zone. Women who take motherhood seriously simply don't have unlimited career options. Instead of a heart devoted to family, there can be a head consumed with getting ahead by earning more and achieving more in order to spend more and enjoy more perks. The enticement to earn, spend, accumulate, and amass it all right now is consuming the American public. Without doubt, the primary concern for American parents seems to be *time*. They feel hurried and rushed every day. They wake up tired and go to bed wired. They are on the fast track and don't see an exit. Nurturing a child physically, emotionally, and spiritually is in itself a consuming task that some would call a "career."

Postmodernism does not have a child-friendly message. Parents are losing their children. Individualism has driven them inward, letting selfishness reign; materialism has captured their hearts so that things are more important than people; and violence plagues them even in the school classroom as the lack of virtue and discipline overtakes their peers. This self-centered ideology suggests that there are many socially approved and legitimate *right* ways of doing things, and the *right* way is to be determined by personal choice or community consensus.

Metal detectors and security guards aren't enough to protect the nation's children. Public schools across the nation are cautiously returning to *character education* in their already beleaguered curriculums out of the frustration that some parents aren't doing a very good job of teaching morals or virtues to their children. But many parents still believe that children need limits and whatever discipline is necessary to help them honor those boundaries. They want their children to have good character, but they are overwhelmed with how to do the job.

Children must learn early that the individual is not the final arbiter of what is right and wrong. Bouncing against the walls erected by parents should send children back to center. Whatever boundaries have been erected should help them prepare for happy and productive lives. Lessons in responsibility and accountability, discipline and self-restraint, and the reciprocity of interpersonal relationships are best taught by parents within the security of the family circle.

HOPE FOR THE FUTURE

A report from Wirthlin Worldwide polling expresses support for the traditional family: 84 percent agreed that marriage is defined as "one man and one woman"; 78 percent believed that families are the "fundamental unit of society"; 86 percent of non-U.S. respondents said that children should be reared by a married mother and father; 64 percent would center a hypothetical new society around "family" instead of other choices like government, business, church, or the individual.

Because the family is a natural institution, established by the Creator God and made up of human beings created by God and endowed with certain unalienable rights that cannot be denied by government, they do not exist to serve the state, nor is the state assigned to rule the family. Instead government should recognize and respect the natural family just as they should recognize and respect basic human rights.

Although the idea of family often becomes a political football, falling victim to oversimplification and idealism from some proponents or to skewing and distortion by others, the fact remains that families are the bedrock of society regardless of cultural or ethnic setting. Despite the lack of understanding of what God designed the family to be and the confusion engendered by social and cultural influences that even contradict the basic principles of morality, the design for marriage and parenthood described in the Bible has found its way into society where it is being understood and appreciated by many people all over the world. The family is to be the seedbed for character building and for virtues upon which a successful society depends. *Good families are the product of months of endless mundane tasks, years of painstaking nurture, and seasons of personal sacrifice.* Families will sail through stormy seas; but if parents chart the course well, the record confirms amazing consistency in a passage to safe harbor. Children ought to be the one investment and legacy parents can leave behind to tell the world what they themselves were really like!

POLITICALLY CORRECT DEFINITIONS

The United Nations has been attempting to redefine the family as whatever anyone wants it to be. Everyone is invited to define family boundaries according to his own preferences or cultural and social forms. Partners of the same gender, polygamous or community groupings, two hobos around a campfire, and even creatures from outer space would qualify.

Even some of the most liberal social engineers understand that the family is the fundamental building block for all societies and the most effective tool for social change. What kind of tool is another question—a shock absorber to cushion the upheaval, an engine to drive into society new ideas and models or a rope or chain to hold us to the foundations already laid. If the family breaks down, what institution can ever put society back together again!

The problem with *chameleon definitions* begins with the confusion engendered. There is no structure, order, or law without definitions at the foundation. If you can redefine the family to mean *any* group of people related to one another in *any* way, the term becomes meaningless to this generation as well as to those to come.

Even the government cannot escape the awesome influence of the family. The Universal Declaration of Human Rights adopted in 1948 had these powerful affirmations of the family:

- The unqualified right to life of all individuals
- The reality of family autonomy in relationship to the state
- The absolute right of men and women "of full age" to unite in marriage and procreate without interference from the state
- The fundamental place of the family as deserving protection from any who would seek to undermine it
- The linkage of family and liberty to property ownership
- The moral imperative of a "family wage" as opposed to the necessity of two incomes to support the family
- The special status of mothers and children in social, cultural, or government policy
- The "prior right" of parents to direct the education of their children.[2]

Even those who seek to redefine the family for their own purposes want to see an obligation on the part of parents to fulfill their responsibility to rear their own children. God, not the government and not the church or any religious institution, assigned to parents this responsibility, and God above all others holds them accountable.[3]

CULTURALLY CONDITIONED CHANGES

How did families in the past manage with only one breadwinner? Statistics provide interesting information. First, in dollars and cents, husbands who are sole providers, are averaging

30 percent more in today's buying power than their 1960 counterparts. In two-income marriages, that earning power jumps even higher, giving modern couples twice the real income (i.e., twice the buying power, allowing for inflation and differences in the cost of living) of their 1960 counterparts.

Expectations, not insufficient family income, are the problem. Families lived much more simply in past years; the average-size house has nearly doubled since the 1950s. The enhancements in tastes and standards of living have carried a hefty price tag. Purchases of beef per capita went from 85 to 104 pounds; the number of households with dishwashers jumped from 7 to 43 percent, with clothes dryers from 20 to 62 percent, and even with electric can openers from 5 to 64 percent; two-car families increased from 16 to 56 percent.

Children, too, have become a more expensive item in the budget. Parents expect to outfit their offspring in designer clothing and equip them with personal computers, sporting goods, and automobiles even before they complete high school. Americans have improved their quality of life not only in material terms but also in terms of socially and intellectually broadening experiences.[4]

Blended families have been around in some form since the days of the Old Testament when polygamous unions brought together children who had the same father but different mothers. The blended family is now defined as a family formed when two persons marry and at least one of them has custody of a child or children from a previous relationship. Sometimes the blended family is formed upon the death of a spouse, but more likely it is the result of divorce or broken homes. These families need all the help they can get to forge ties that will hold the more complex family structure together. The most frequently surfacing problems in blended homes involve children and the complexities of producing a cohesiveness between two (often diametrically opposite) family systems and of establishing family bonds in the midst of natural jealousies and the insecurities that accompany traumatic change.

PRAGMATIC PRACTICES

The family is in effect a small civilization, a microcosm of society. Therefore, if the family is sick and dying, the society made up of those families will become ill and begin the slow and agonizing death that follows.

Chester E. Finn Jr., formerly a professor of education and public policy at Vanderbilt University and now at the Manhattan Institute, added his concern for the survival of the traditional family: "With rare exceptions, two-parent families are good for children, one-parent families are bad, zero-parent families are horrible." This professor speaks pragmatically from what he has observed as an educator in the arena of public policy. The growing incidence of divorce and unwed motherhood has reduced the amount of money available to spend on children. The decline and disintegration of the family has left more children emotionally disturbed and psychologically distressed.

Women seem to feel more freedom to bear and rear children without getting married. The maternal instinct buried within a woman's nature asserts itself *without* the tempering of boundaries. If a woman wants a child without the encumbrance of a husband, she finds a way through overt promiscuity or covert surrogate childbearing to get a child on her own.

Couples divorce and remarry on a whim so that the number of broken and patched-together families is beyond what could have been comprehended even two decades ago. I was amazed to read that only 25 to 30 percent of divorces are initiated by husbands. The majority of marriages end because of a wife's action.[5] Self-fulfillment seems to have moved into prominence. Spouses focus on themselves and their desires rather than obligations to the family. Studies still show overwhelmingly that children of divorce suffer—in academic work, in propensity to delinquency, in substance abuse, in promiscuity—and they are more susceptible to ending their own marriages.

Tragically, divorce actually redefines marriage. It tears the heart out of the *covenant*[6] (a spiritual, as well as legal, document), which by definition goes beyond a contract (a legal document). In both covenant and contract, the parties involved make a commitment for their respective personal benefit. However, with the latter document, when the parties involved feel the arrangement has served its purpose, they are quick to find ways to abrogate the contract and move beyond its mutual obligations. A contract is easily negotiated, renegotiated, and even rescinded, according to the whim of those involved.

On the other hand, a covenant assumes a unique and intimate relationship between the parties. It is described as a formal, solemn commitment intended as absolutely binding. In the Old Testament, the covenant was a seal on the relationship between God and His chosen people Israel.[7] Marriage became the metaphor or paradigm used to illustrate that unique relationship. In the New Testament, the same metaphor described the relationship between Christ and His church.[8]

No wonder God "hate[s] divorce."[9] To accept divorce as an option is to say by default that marriage was never binding. The "one-flesh" concept becomes meaningless, or amputation is deemed better than wholeness. Popular Christian vocalist Amy Grant and country music megastar Vince Gill dumped their respective spouses. Grant had the chutzpah to say that she knew God hated divorce (it *is* recorded in Scripture), but she looked to higher, *"freeing* truth" truth based on a counselor's words that "God made marriage for people. He didn't make people for marriage. . . . If you have two people that are not thriving healthily in a situation, I say remove the marriage."[10]

Such reasoning is to suggest that marriage exists merely for the benefit of an individual, not necessarily for the spouse or children and certainly not for the glory of God. Decisions are made based on personal feelings and not on what is clearly written in the Word of God. When commitment to marriage becomes meaningless, self-fulfillment becomes more important than self-sacrifice; self-centeredness replaces other-person concerns; self-will overshadows God-directed purposes and plans; personally envisioned happiness rises above God-defined holiness.

This generation has witnessed the collapse of any national consensus on how to define the family and how to order its workings. A deep chasm has developed between behavior (what you do) and ideology (what you believe). Your personal behavior must be brought into conformity with what you believe, or you sacrifice your beliefs on the altar of expediency, willing to go along to get along with whatever the current fads may be.

Contemplating the pragmatic practices that have sought to refashion the family is a reminder that individuals ultimately are not willing to be reshaped according to the whims of politicians and theoreticians. The natures of men and women, who are the creation of God, are marked by certain constants. Men and women by divine design have the longing for a lifelong commitment in marriage; a parent and child have an intrinsic bond; they naturally long for independent households of their own. These common human desires are prerequisites for personal liberty and social order. Solving social problems begins with restoring families as the basic unit in society and encouraging those families to teach their children self-discipline, personal responsibility, and moral restraint.

THE TIME-TESTED BIBLICAL DEFINITION

If you really want to go back to the earliest documents and most fundamental definition of the family, then the Bible is a good place to start. Its definition is brief and concise. There is no ambiguity or confusion. Human judgment is there, but these individual subjective choices are overshadowed by divine objectivity.

God defined the family as the foundational institution of human society. Before there were civil governments or assemblies of worship of any kind, God established the home in the Garden of Eden. He created the man and the woman and then brought them together. They were to forge a unique companionship with each other; they were to exercise dominion over the world God had created; they were to continue the generations by linking hands with God Himself in procreation; and they were to praise and worship God. From the beginning, God has used the family as the primary classroom and as the foremost object lesson for teaching men and women about Himself and for challenging them to the holy lifestyle He demands.

All other institutions were built around the family. The family has been envisioned as the *first church,* the place where basic spiritual truths are taught; the *first school,* the base for laying foundations for wisdom and learning or education; the *first state,* an environment in which conformity to law and order is demanded from a child in lieu of punishment for evildoing or disobedience. Families make up communities. They form the membership of churches, and they create a demand for educational centers.

At the beginning of creation, a "garden," suggesting a place "covered" or "hidden" or "hedged around" was the first home.[11] This sheltered place named "Eden," from a root meaning "delight," contained everything the man and woman needed for happy and prosperous living—food and water, beauty and companionship.[12]

In whatever setting, a garden brings memories of a set-apart area, usually with verdant and living greenery, perhaps beautiful and fragrant flowers, and often lush vegetation. There you will find both sunshine and shade with a good measure of solitude or quiet for a garden paradise. This combination of beauty and utility is unique and much to be desired.

A garden of sheltered beauty requires planning and preparation. Its reward can be pleasure for you, fellowship with others, and even a retreat to God for those willing to spend the time and make the commitment. God's choice of the garden metaphor to describe the first and only perfect home is no coincidence. This initial home in Eden was unmarred by sin and untouched by evil.

The family was God's idea and not a human invention to be adapted by a nation or a cultural phenomenon to be embraced by a particular generation. God designed the home to be the foundation of the world He created. Because the family is not merely the result of a natural inclination originating with human ingenuity, its success does not come automatically to anyone who enters its borders by birth, adoption, or commitment. To make a family work efficiently and effectively requires faithful determination, loving commitment, and dedicated service on the part of all its members one to the other.

The family, by divine design, meets the physical, emotional, intellectual, and spiritual needs of both men and women in every season of life. The family is not a temporary, stop-gap solution to loneliness; it is not a buffet of choices for fun and entertainment; it is not a vehicle for respectability and community status. The strength of the family lies in the exclusive commitment of those within its circle to one another, in the permanent and lasting ties among its members, and in the selfless, loving service administered by each to the other.

The Bible is permeated with the family. The book of Genesis presents God's plan for the relationship of the man and woman in marriage.[13] Each of the Ten Commandments found in the Decalogue affects the family circle.[14] In Leviticus, the Laws of Israel contain the death penalty for anyone who prostitutes the home.[15] In Numbers, the census or numbering of the people is done by families.[16] Deuteronomy has an extensive discussion on parental instruction.[17]

The book of Joshua is a biography of a godly patriarch who led his family and nation to follow the God of Israel.[18] The book of Judges records the consequences of unbridled lust.[19] Ruth contains an example of familial devotion within the extended family as well as one of the most beautiful stories of romantic love and committed marriage found in all of literature.[20]

In the historical books of Samuel, Kings, and Chronicles, the influence of the family upon the lives of kings is clearly noted.[21] The devotion and spiritual sensitivity of the prophet Samuel is attributed in part to his godly mother Hannah.[22] The wickedness of King Ahab was magnified and extended by his wife Jezebel.[23] In Ezra, Nehemiah, and Esther, godly generations are preserved because of the strength of the family.[24]

Job experienced Satan's most vicious attack on his home through the death of his children, through the disease that afflicted him personally, through the poverty he experienced after losing his household and possessions, and through the internal strife in his marriage.[25] The book of Psalms contains many promises of blessings for the family committed to the Lord.[26] Proverbs is a book devoted to family living and interpersonal relationships.[27] Ecclesiastes, too, abounds with the importance of intimacy with God in all relationships, including the family circle.[28] The Song of Solomon is an explicit record of an exclusive, monogamous love between a man and a woman committed to each other.[29]

The prophetic books are also full of allusions to families. In addition, the metaphor of the family provides an object lesson for God to reveal Himself to the human family in terms they could easily understand. Consequences for open violation of godly principles within families are clearly presented.[30]

In the New Testament, the family continued to be a means of communication between God and His creation. In Matthew, Mark, Luke, and John, Jesus presented His own teachings concerning the family and relationships within its circle.[31] In fact, the first miracle of Jesus took place at a wedding in Cana.[32] The book of Acts notes the home, as well as the synagogue, as a center for worship.[33] The Epistles written by the apostles also abound in teachings concerning the family.[34] Even the Apocalypse uses the metaphor of marriage, with allusions to the bride and Bridegroom, to deliver its message.[35]

CONCLUSION

What is a home? Is it a residential hotel—a house with the latest comforts and a big mortgage? Is it a short-order restaurant—a filling station for refueling? Is it any network of support where you find love and encouragement? Is it a passageway to life—a place to hang your coat and hat as you pass through the seasons of life?

Perhaps Americans need to become less concerned with luxuries and more interested in the intangible joy coming from time spent with their families. Families need to recapture their role in providing emotional and moral sustenance. They ought to reign as a source of strength. The government-sponsored health system doesn't deliver what it has promised; the political system doesn't give you the representation or participation you want; the legal system doesn't give you the justice for which your heart longs; even the churches and religious leaders don't have as many answers to your family's problems as you desire.

The *compass plant* is similar in appearance to a sunflower, but it has a special function for hikers. The plant's leaves point north and south in order to avoid being dried by the sun. The family serves the same purpose in the divine economy. It is far more effective than government officials, educators, employers, or even religious leaders in imparting the values and virtues demanded for high and lofty living. Marriage is an exceptional, exclusive relationship in which one man and one woman—two biologically distinct individuals—are welded into one mysterious union. They together have the assignment of continuing the generations. Parents are best equipped to teach their children and young people to live up to their own responsibilities and to have respect for others. Such teaching is best done in the midst of supportive loving relationships within the family. The key role of the family is the design of God Himself.

You who are committed to home and family should be encouraged to know that what you do for God may not appear in the earth's *times*, but those deeds will be recorded in heaven's *eternities*. The family is a project worth taking on!

1. Frank Swoboda, "Split Schedules Add Stress on Women," *News & Observer,* 10 March 2000.

2. Allan Carlson, opening remarks to the World Congress of Families II, Geneva, Switzerland, 14–17 November 1999.

3. Deut. 6:4–9; Eph. 6:4.

4. A Newsday Service, "Major Shifts in Tastes and Standards Seen in U.S.," an excerpt from Andrew Hacker, *U/S: A Statistical Portrait of the American People,* (New York: Viking Press, 1983).

5. Susan Orr, "Real Women Stay Married," *Washington Watch* 11 (June 2000): 1.

6. Hebrew *berith.*

7. Isa. 54:5.

8. Eph. 5:21–33.

9. Mal. 2:16.

10. Glenn Stanton, "Divorce: Bible Belt Style," *Focus on the Family,* June 2000, 18–20.

11. In the Bible the home is described as a "garden" (Hebrew *gan*); Gen. 2:8.

12. Gen. 2:8–10; 3:8.

13. Gen. 2:24.

14. Exod. 20:1–17.

15. Lev. 20:9–21.

16. Num. 1:2.

17. Deut. 6:1–12.

18. Josh. 24:15.

19. Judg. 13–16.

20. Ruth 1–4.

21. 1 Kings 22:51–53.

22. 1 Sam. 1:27–28.

23. 1 Kings 21:5–16.

24. Esther 2:20; 4:14.

25. Job 1:13–21; 2:7–10.

26. Ps. 127.

27. Prov. 14:1; 22:6.

28. Eccl. 4:9–12.

29. Song of Sol. 4:1–7.

30. Isa. 3:12–26; Jer. 31:29–30; Lam. 4:10; Ezek. 16:44–45; Hos. 4:1–5; Joel 2:28–29; Mic. 7:5–6; Mal. 2:14–16.

31. Matt. 19:3–9.

32. John 2:1–11.

33. Acts 2:46; 12:12.

34. 1 Cor. 11:1–16; Eph. 5:21–6:4; Col. 3:18–21; 1 Thess. 4:1–7; 1 Tim. 3:1–12; Titus 2:1–5; Heb. 12:5–11; 1 Pet. 3:1–7.

35. Rev. 19:7.

2

Does the Bible Really Say That?

HOME MAY BE A SPACIOUS AND LUXURIOUS PALACE; it may be a tiny nondescript cottage, or anything in between. Home is not where you board for a while or visit occasionally or time-share regularly enough to be familiar with its rooms and cozy corners. Rather the front-door key is in your pocket. On a whim, you can sit before the glow of a fire you build with your own kindling. Your presence pervades the whole house, and it is home precisely because you are there. Home is where love lives, and that love will bring a crowning touch like nothing else.

From the Jewish roots of the Old Testament to the Christian admonitions of the New Testament, the Bible offers some clear and precise directives concerning the family. Husbands and fathers are reminded to lead their families.[1] They are also to love their wives and children unselfishly,[2] and they are to labor faithfully in providing for their families[3] as well as protecting them.[4] Husbands and fathers are called to "servant leadership"—giving responsible direction to the family, while ministering to the needs of each family member with unselfish sensitivity.

Wives and mothers have the responsibility of submitting to their own husbands[5] by supporting their leadership in the family.[6] They also have the assignment of loving their husbands and children and providing nurturing care within the family.[7] Children are not without responsibilities. They are to honor and obey their parents.[8]

GET THE FACTS

Marriage does matter. A strong family starts with a steadfast marriage. The marital love shared between one man and one woman is the greatest relationship human beings can have. God designed this shared love to be the channel for procreation of human life, yielding the consummate responsibility— a child. By whatever measure—economic, social, educational, and spiritual—the evidence proves that two parents living and functioning together are better than one. A strong marriage begins with a foundation of faithfulness between husband and wife, which is expressed through spiritual and legal covenant in a public wedding ceremony. Each is the creation of God, and both are described in the biblical Creation account as being "in His image."[9] Both have functions to perform in the world schema as they share in dominion over the world God created. However, *identical* is not a synonym for *equal*. You don't achieve equality by merely mimicking or doing the same thing as another.

Wives cannot reach their full potential if they are trying to imitate their husbands, just as husbands cannot attain their full productivity if they are concerned about doing the same tasks as their wives. In this responsibility for overseeing the world, the roles of husbands and wives are to be complementary. They are to fit together so that each enhances and extends the other.

This complementarity certainly extends to the family. The father devotes his primary energies to provide the necessities of life for his wife and children. The mother gives herself to keeping the home and nurturing the children, since someone must assume responsibility for protecting the young as they prepare to take their places in society.

The mutuality of husband and wife as a couple is not to exclude either from a particular contribution to the family; nor does it suggest they are to perform the same tasks. Rather they are to work together as a team, mutually committed to dominion of the earth and to the preparation of the next generation. Emphasis is not on the individual and his own interests and well-being, but rather on the commitment of the couple to each other and to the family and its nurture.

The crux of the matter is that God designed the differences between a man and a woman so they would complement and complete each other. In fact, the difference dividing one from the other also cements a man and woman into the covenant of marital love and commitment, which they then share with the children who come from their loving union.

FOLLOW THE MANUAL

God's plan for marriage is presented in Scripture.[10] He reveals purposes for marriage: intimate companionship,[11] sexual fulfillment,[12] responsible parenthood,[13] family solidarity and unity,[14] spiritual teaching.[15]

Marriage is a covenant commitment to the exclusive and permanent union of one man and one woman. God's purpose for bringing together a man and a woman in marriage was introduced at the time of Creation[16] and then reaffirmed by Jesus in the Gospels and by Paul in the Epistles.[17] God's principle for marriage transcends time and culture. Marriage is not a flexible contract between consenting human beings. Rather, the strong and enduring bond of marriage, pledged in the presence of God Himself, is enriched by the couple's unconditional love for and acceptance of each other.

In marriage, a husband and wife physically become one flesh. Such a union is designed to provide a lifetime of spiritual and emotional support,[18] to offer a channel for the mutual satisfaction of sexual desires, and to present the best setting for conceiving and nurturing the next generation. The complementary relationship between husband and wife is presented as part of the garden paradise before the Fall interrupted their perfect setting. This relationship is then carefully defined within the canon of Scripture for succeeding generations.[19]

Monogamy is absolutely the divine plan.[20] Scripture calls for a man to "be united to his wife," *not his wives!* Fidelity is expected to be the norm.[21] Sexual purity is demanded. Scripture issues a clear warning against all perverted sexual behavior. Not only is heterosexuality the plan of the Creator, but homosexuality and bestiality are boldly condemned.[22]

Complementarity marks the relationship of a husband and wife who are both created in the image of God, who are both equally His children, and who both come to Him in the same way. They are expected to exercise dominion over the world in complementary ways. *Through the covenant of marriage, committed people become cooperative partners, who then are prepared to become conscientious parents!* The commitment of husband and wife is to cling to God's plan for the family with tenacity, to love one another unconditionally, and to pursue life with the fear of the Lord in their hearts.[23] *The relationship is marked by contrast and reciprocity: The husband is a servant leader and the wife is a gracious helper.*

THE INFRASTRUCTURE OF MARRIAGE

The Jews throughout history have held the marriage covenant as high and holy. The *Ketubah*[24] required from the Jewish groom was to be read aloud during the marriage ceremony.

The document was often decorated with creativity and skill—
an artistic masterpiece.

My *Ketubah* was an anniversary gift from my husband.
The treasured document was designed by Marcia Kaniel, an
official Israeli scribe. Her beautiful calligraphy penned in
Aramaic, the official language used for Jewish documents, is
itself a work of art. Its enhancing border is an ornamental
design found in excavations of the ancient Herodian Temple.
This exquisite piece of art hanging beside my wedding portrait reminds me of my husband's love.

Most people are not surprised to learn that the *Ketubah*
was and remains a one-sided contract, but they are shocked
that *the document details the husband's responsibilities to his
wife during their life together.* The legalities associated with
the *Ketubah* were formulated by Jewish sages based upon
explicit instructions found in the Old Testament.[25] Not only
were husbands commanded to provide food, clothing, and
conjugal rights to their wives, but they were also to respect
them. The word *serve* was also found repeatedly in this document designed to protect the wife and ensure provision for
her needs. The groom had to sign the document, but the
bride's signature was optional since she was *receiving* the
commitment.[26]

More and more Americans are choosing not to marry.
Others marry later, exit marriage more quickly, or choose to
live together before marriage, in between marriages, after marriage, or even as an alternative to marriage. Marriage is losing
much of its legal, social, and religious authority. What has
taken its place is a *couple relationship* that provides for sexual
and emotional gratification. The absence of covenant commitment between a husband and wife suggests a lack of genuine
love or concern for each other and an absence of responsibility
to anyone else—even the children born to their union![27]

Considerable scientific evidence suggests that more psychological damage is done by voluntary breakup of the family through divorce than by involuntary breakup caused by death.[28] Government adds to the havoc brought on by divorce by arbitrarily denying reality. States are already declaring that the marriage covenant can be immediately and unilaterally broken by either spouse for any or no reason. Such frivolous dissolution makes the marriage commitment less binding than any other recognized contract in society. It comes close to abolishing legal recognition of the marital union.

Happy couples communicate well. They are compatible and have worked out ways to deal with conflict. They are emotionally close and feel connected. Even their leisure activities regularly overlap. They have flexibility in their relationship; they can change and adapt when necessary. They work at building strengths as a couple. Life is a series of storms with deadlines and competition that stretch and even tear apart. An intimate marriage can offer a safe harbor where a couple can drop anchor and ride out the storm by being available and offering comfort to each other.

Commitment is the foundation for marriage. Yet more and more is missing from the modern marriage ceremony. Dozens of self-help or do-it-yourself software kits for dissolving marriage are found on the Internet. Someone suggested that almost three thousand titles on divorce were posted on one of the online bookstores. It is tragic to think that divorce is just a book or software kit away. Some sociologists have flippantly referred to marriage as an impermanent relationship and to divorce as "serial monogamy."

Marriage, according to God's plan, is a lifelong commitment. The breaking of its bonds brings hurt to all involved, and thus every effort ought to be made for marital reconciliation and restoration.[29] The rabbis were divided on the matter of divorce. Followers of Rabbi Shammai argued that divorce should only be granted when adultery had occurred; followers of Rabbi Hillel held that divorce was permitted for virtually any reason.

Jesus during His ministry rejected both of these rabbinic interpretations of the Mosaic Law.[30] Rather, He referred to Creation and the giving of the biblical plan for marriage presented in the book of Genesis.[31] He noted that the "hardness" of the human heart could on occasion circumvent that plan.[32] It is impossible to understand Jesus' position on divorce unless you recognize His commitment to permanent monogamy as presented in Genesis and reaffirmed in the New Testament.

Moses did not issue a "command" for divorce but rather made such an allowance for situations in which wives might be abused by unscrupulous husbands. Some religious leaders of the first century had taken the "permission" of the Law as given by Moses and turned it into a "command" in which human mistakes and inadequacies became a couple's justification for circumventing God's plan for marriage.

Jesus never taught that an innocent party wronged in marital infidelity must divorce an unfaithful spouse! The binding commitment at the heart of marriage never depends on what you want or what your partner does or doesn't do. God's plan does not depend on perfect people or the right circumstances. Instead He gives a perfect plan that works even in the midst of human imperfections.

The kinship bond between husbands and wives and between parents and children is the same permanent and binding covenant bond that God makes with His creation. To break that bond is to destroy the metaphor God has chosen to reveal the kind of relationship He wants to have with His children. God hates divorce, and He does not choose the

dissolution of a marriage for anyone.[33] Nevertheless, whenever divorce happens, God works redemptively. Anyone who
seeks His forgiveness will be reconciled to Him; and with
God, forgiveness is as if it never happened.

When sin entered the Garden of Eden, distortions came
into the relationships between men and women. Chaos and
tragedy spread throughout the world. A husband's loving,
humble headship has often been replaced with tyrannical
domination or indifferent passivity. A wife's voluntary and
willing submission has often been exchanged for usurpation
of authority or servility. Redemption in Christ would call for
husbands to forsake harsh or selfish leadership and to extend
loving care to their wives. At the same time, wives are asked
to forsake resistance to the authority of their respective
husbands and to practice willing, joyful submission to the
leadership of their husbands.[34] *For both the husband and wife
this is a choice: A husband must choose to use his power in a
loving servant leadership; a wife must choose to put aside her
power to accept that leadership. Each is giving up and not
grasping for.*

Intact marriages are important to children, who have a
profound sense of abandonment, loss, and rejection when
they lose a parent. Growing up in a single-parent household is
tough on children.

If one parent leaves, a child may live forever with the fear
that the other parent will also disappear. This emotional strain
often prompts poor performance in school, defiance of authorities, barriers to lasting friendships, exhibitions of aggressive-
ness, or tendencies to isolation. "No-fault" divorce, usually
accompanied by the father's absence from the home, has
increased poverty and insecurity for women and children.

THE ROLE OF THE HUSBAND

God commands husbands to love their wives as Christ loved the church.[35] This love is protective, nurturing, serving, and edifying. It is not overshadowed or replaced with, but accompanied by, headship. Headship calls the husband to a loving leadership in which he cares responsibly for his wife's spiritual, emotional, and physical needs.

The husband's headship was established by God before the Fall, after which Adam and Eve were expelled from their garden paradise. Headship was not the result of sin.[36] Responsibility for leadership in the home is to be assumed with humility and a servant's heart. It is not a right to be grasped with pride and demanded through tyranny. The wife is to respond to her husband's loving headship with honor and respect.[37]

Servanthood does not nullify leadership but rather defines and refines its outworking. The balance between servanthood and leadership is beautifully portrayed in Jesus Himself as He modeled servant leadership for the husband and selfless submission for the wife.[38] Not only did Jesus model the Creator's plan for different roles, but He also affirmed the equality in Christ of the husband and the wife.[39] As the wife submits herself to her husband's leadership, the husband humbles himself to meet his wife's needs for love and nurture.[40]

The major responsibility of the husband in marriage as expressed in the New Testament is to love his wife as Christ loved the church.[41] *Love* is an active verb.[42] Such love does not describe a romantic feeling; rather, it testifies to a heart commitment. The example given by the apostle Paul is clear because he challenges husbands to love their wives as Jesus loved the church. Jesus died for the church. A love that puts your life on the line is self-sacrificing.

An emergency hospitalization put me out of circulation immediately prior to my husband's annual faculty retreat. There were complications with my surgery. Although my sister, who is a nurse, was in constant attendance, I really needed my husband's emotional support and spiritual encouragement. From the time I entered surgery throughout the succeeding week of intensive care, Paige did not leave the hospital. He slept on a cot; he ate hospital food; he canceled his Sunday preaching assignment; he conducted his retreat and took care of other responsibilities via the telephone and other administrators. I needed him, and he was there. I have never doubted that humanly speaking Paige considered me—not his job, his preaching ministry, his colleagues, the rest of the family—to be his first priority!

The apostle Paul includes the admonition that husbands are to encourage their wives to reach their greatest potential.[43] My own academic preparation would have ended with a baccalaureate degree if it had not been for the vision and determination of my husband. Allergies, asthma, and multiple bouts with pneumonia plagued me during those school years. I never felt well; my body required lengthy periods of bed rest. School simply was not high on my list of priorities! But my husband felt that I had unique potential academically. He insisted that I pursue graduate work, and he has been my resident teacher and mentor through all my academic pursuits. I would not have completed any of my graduate degrees except for his persistent encouragement. I think I am living and working *beyond* my potential—whatever that may be—and I have Paige Patterson to thank!

The apostle Peter admonishes a husband to live with his wife in a personalized understanding of her needs and even her desires.[44] My husband has never stopped studying me through almost four decades of marriage. He knows what

I like; he is aware of my favorite colors; he can pick out clothing (more challenging with aging and pounds!); he can select beautiful jewelry. He knows how much I adore fresh-cut flowers.

One Mother's Day a large and beautiful spring bouquet with fragrant roses was delivered to me. We had miles to travel before returning to Magnolia Hill, yet Paige indulged me by carefully carrying the arrangement in and out of hotel rooms so that I would not have to leave it behind. Those flowers brought me fragrant joy for two weeks!

Paige knows that I would rather have afternoon tea than just about anything else, and we have indulged in that restful pastime literally around the world—throughout England, in Scotland, Wales, New Zealand, Australia, South Africa, Zimbabwe, Singapore, Hong Kong, Bangkok, Jerusalem, Hawaii, Istanbul, the Jakarta airport, and a host of other places. I remember our favorite—Chinese afternoon tea in Hong Kong with fragrant chrysanthemum Jasmine tea and dim-sum-style accompaniments!

A husband is to respect and esteem his wife. Interestingly, if a husband fails to treat his wife with dignity and to love her sacrificially, he not only risks damaging his relationship to his wife, but he also hinders his relationship with God.[45] God will turn a deaf ear to any husband who fails to treat his wife with loving respect. Anyone observing my husband is aware of his respect for me. He is undoubtedly the head of our household. He makes decisions when we come to an impasse in our discussions on whatever the matter. However, he is almost always careful to ask me for my views and observations, and he weighs what I say before making his final decision. Often he decides in my favor, but he may also choose another way. Yet he genuinely wants to hear from me. Any feedback becomes my gift to Paige—no manipulating how it's used and no snatching it back. What I give to him is then his to use as he sees fit!

There have been times when he probably wishes he had not listened to me and other times when he wishes that he had given more attention to my concerns. When we were in the university, Paige was pastor of a congregation struggling with overwhelming indebtedness. For a time we received no regular salary. We lived in a parsonage adjoining the church, and the people were generous with their garden produce.

Paige announced that he needed a football for the church youth program. I pleaded with him not to spend our meager funds and made suggestions on alternative entertainment. But Paige purchased a football—and the most expensive one! I was devastated. He assured me that God would provide!

On Sunday afternoon when Paige went out to the yard between our house and the church to play football with the young people, he began with a beautiful spiral kick. However, the ball's landing happened to be on a rosebush. A large thorn caught the ball, and in minutes it was losing air. The football could not be repaired; the extravagant purchase was gone before a game could be played.

God is much more effective than wives in teaching lessons to husbands, and the Lord always has something to be learned by wives in the process. No unexpected funds entered our bank account in the succeeding weeks. We suffered together in stretching an already inadequate budget to absorb the loss, but we survived; and we both learned!

THE ROLE OF THE WIFE

Wives were created to be "helpers" to their husbands.[46] A wife's submission to her husband does not decrease her worth but rather enhances her value to her husband and to the Lord.[47] This humble and voluntary yielding of a wife to her husband's leadership becomes a means of drawing her husband to God, a channel for spiritual growth as the wife ultimately trusts herself to the Lord, and a means to bring honor to His Word.[48]

According to an article in the *Washington Times,* more women support the family paradigm in which the husband takes leadership and holds the primary role of provider. Forty-eight percent of the respondents affirmed that society would be better if husbands sought achievement in their employment and wives looked for satisfaction in their work in the home.[49]

Another study noted that the health of a husband whose wife is employed full-time outside the home declines by more than 25 percent. On the other hand, a wife's health was not affected by the same amount of work by her husband. The researcher suggested the "subtle factors" at work in a marriage. For example, a wife would have less time to encourage and facilitate "a number of things that reduce stress and promote health and manage illness" if she were committed to full-time employment.[50]

The phrase "helper comparable to him" describes the woman God created to become a partner with the man in the overwhelming task of exercising dominion over the world and extending the generations.[51] The word *helper* has no hint of inferiority and is used by God to describe Himself. It denotes function rather than worth.[52] I, as a helper to my husband and mother to my children, make each family member more successful by supporting them through my tasks in the home. I work hard at making our home the best place to be for everyone!

The woman is also identified as one "comparable to him [the man]."[53] She is like and equal to the man in her person even though different from him and unique in her function.

This descriptive word (Heb. *kenegdo*) emphasizes the commonality of the man and the woman. The woman was neither inferior nor superior to the man, but she corresponded to him in such a way as to make it possible for them to have the most intimate fellowship. Both were created in the image of God, and each was to have a part in dominion over the earth and continuing the generations.

In the midst of differences in nature and function, women and men need to be conscious of what each can do to respond to the needs of the other. Wives should give attention to their appearance. Even when a wife has been in her grubbies all day, she can prepare for her husband's homecoming with a quick touch-up. Husbands who work hard anticipate the respite of a well-planned, tasty meal, and they appreciate greatly a wife who is sensitive to budget restraints and economy in household planning. A wife also needs to learn when to speak and when to be silent; that's part of being a good friend and companion. She ought to lavish her affection on husband and children. Husbands appreciate a godly woman of strength but not a woman wearing a veneer of prudish sanctity.

Husbands also ought to give attention to their appearance, even when lounging around the house. They please their wives with little thoughtful acts of kindness and by telling them about their work—what they have done and what they have to do. They develop sensitivity to their wives' need for affection; they know when to back off and when to close in. Just telling her *I love you* every day and remembering to kiss her when you leave and when you come home and perhaps a few times in between will pay dividends! Remembering to express gratitude for the investment she makes in routine tasks to keep the home comfortable and to notice when she has done something special will not go unnoticed. She doesn't need unwarranted or insincere praise, but she does need a cloak of protection from discussing her weaknesses in public. Yet all of these things pale before the big one—seeing a man committed to a godly lifestyle who brings a spiritual emphasis to the home with the life he lives as well as the words he says.

Men and women think and respond differently. Although their thoughts and responses may be diametrically opposite, neither is necessarily right or wrong. Rather, together they bring balance and strength to a marriage. You cannot place all men and all women in a rigid stereotype or grid. However, some distinctives in the masculine and feminine natures point the way to a better understanding of each other.

Men are usually more stimulated by what they see, while women tend to be more sensitive to words or physical touch. Men are considered more logical and objective in their judgments, while women tend to reflect more sensitivity and subjectivity in coming to their conclusions.

Men seem overwhelmed with a drive toward quantity, while women are more concerned with quality control. Have you observed the contrast in child care rendered by mothers and fathers? When our children were at home, on rare occasions I would have to be away briefly. The children always delighted in supervision by their father. Of course, he was concerned that they have meals and remain healthy. But what kind of meals they had or how late they stayed up or whether they completed homework assignments or even whether they took daily baths—these were so low on priority as to be nonexistent!

There is a difference in overall task accomplishment and being sure that each step is done in the best possible way. Mothers tend to keep their children on a schedule, including a daily washing down! The children are to eat at appointed times, and the menu is to be nutritious. School work is completed before play, and bedtime is strictly observed. Mothers are determined to develop a quality product, and they seem to know instinctively what it takes to do so.

Whereas men seem inclined to concentrate on goals, women tend to thrive on relationships. In other words, men are more often characterized as power-driven, while women tend to be people-driven. It is no coincidence that women have always dominated the service vocations—nurses, teachers, housekeepers, secretaries. Only feministic rhetoric would suggest that these positions are *inferior*.

Who is more important when you are desperately ill—the doctor who drops in once a day or the nurse who checks on you regularly, administers your medication, cleans you up, and offers encouragement along the way? Who is more important—the principal whose office your child visits when he is in trouble or the classroom teacher who spends the day with your child, instructing him in the rudiments of education and teaching him how to live in the world? Who is more important—the owner of the market and supplier of cleaning products or the woman who takes those products and uses them to prepare your dwelling so that it is clean and inviting? Who is more important—the financier or power broker who owns the retail outlets or the woman who works on the floor explaining the products and helping you know what will suit you best? We are living in a upside-down world. We have forgotten just what is important. No one would say that we don't need doctors or principals or business tycoons, but we should recognize that the vast support force necessary for us to make our contributions is important and worth just as much!

Men are looking for ways to harness emotions, while women want to release and enjoy their emotions. Attendees at men's rallies will respond with *amen* and applause, and there may be *some* tears; but for the most part emotions are held tightly in check. On the other hand, women will laugh and cry in the same hour. Their hearts are tender and responsive. They will weep unashamedly. They'll listen with their hearts, respond with their emotions, and move forward with their wills.

Men tend to move toward a single focus, while women are intent on balancing a multifocused life. How else could you rear children! I don't know any mother who can't do, and even concentrate on, several different tasks at once. Men are more apt to look at the bottom line, while women want all the details. My husband calls me every night and sometimes several times during the day when he is away from home. He is interested in what I am doing, and he wants to know what problems I have encountered. However, he prefers the streamlined version—the facts—and I want to share every detail.

For women, romance is atmosphere and environment and how you live; for men, it is what you do. A man thinks of communicating his love primarily through sexual intimacy; a woman wants to communicate and receive love through tender and continual affection. Though typically a man may be searching for affirming praise and verbal appreciation, a woman is yearning for tender affection and security.

As his "helper," a wife complements her husband through her unique function in the divine economy; as one "comparable to him," she, too, is created "in the image of God." Both bear God's image fully, but each expresses that image in God-ordained ways through manhood or womanhood. Thus, distinctions in masculine and feminine roles are ordained by God as part of the created order.[54] Their differing roles in relating to each other paint a picture of God's nature and how He relates to His people. As the realities of headship and submission are enacted within loving, equal, and complementary male-female roles, the image of God is properly reflected.

For wives, *submit* is just as positive a verb as *love,* which is used to describe the husband's assignment. A wife who submits to her husband supports him, encourages him, and obeys him.[55] She works at being the "helper" God designed her to be. However, modern English does not reflect the full impact of the Greek verb[56] and interjects the connotation of forced subservience. That's one reason scholarly study of the Bible is important. Biblical submission takes on an entirely different connotation. Its reference is not to coercive compliance but rather to the deliberately chosen acquiescence of one to the will of another.

Submission is more than obedience—it is a resting, leaning, trusting, abandoning yourself to another. Submission is more than action; it is an attitude of the will that bends, and willingly so, seeking ways to obey. It is devoid of stubbornness. It begins inside with the will but works outward with purpose. Submission is based upon the confidence that God's way is best. It acknowledges how awesome and capable God is rather than dwelling on how burdensome your husband is. Submission should not be based on what kind of husband you have but on what kind of God you serve.

The Old Testament presents examples of women who chose to submit alongside portraits of women who determined to go their own ways. Sarah chose to trust God even when her husband Abraham proved untrustworthy. Abraham identified Sarah as his sister.[57] Although Sarah was his half sister, the daughter of his father but not his mother, she was also his wife.

Pharaoh admired Sarah's beauty and took her to his house under the pretense that she was Abraham's sister. Abraham had put Sarah's purity and her life at risk when he allowed her to go into Pharaoh's court. God intervened with plagues on the household of Pharaoh so that the Egyptian monarch returned Sarah to Abraham.[58] When Abraham repeated his deceptive actions, being more concerned with saving his own life than protecting his wife, Sarah also willingly lied to Abimelech, king of Gerar. Again she was taken into a pagan harem, and once more God intervened and delivered Sarah.[59]

In contrast, Isaac's wife Rebekah put her confidence in her own devices. She feared God could not fulfill His own prophecy concerning Jacob,[60] the son whom she evidently believed had the best spiritual sensitivities. Therefore, she deceived her husband and refused to submit to his leadership concerning the division of inheritance between their two sons. As a result, she brought into her home favoritism, rivalry, and contention. Rebekah's deceit must have broken the intimate fellowship she had enjoyed with a husband who had loved her devotedly and exclusively. She was also permanently separated from Jacob, the son she favored, as well as being estranged from Esau, who had been the victim of her partiality.[61]

Submission is not presented in the Bible as a privilege earned by favored husbands but rather as a responsibility assigned to godly wives. This responsibility is clearly defined by God Himself in the New Testament. It is clearly *voluntary;* that is, self-imposed. Husbands cannot require or demand it; submission must be freely given. It is not inferiority, just as headship is not domination. Before marriage the man and woman stand equal before God; both are made in His image. In marriage, the wife voluntarily becomes submissive to her own husband. The husband then praises his wife for being worthy of his loving devotion.

Genuine submission is also complete and continual. Obeying only requests you consider *reasonable* becomes selfish license and meaningless acquiescence. Biblical submission is to put all of yourself—your energies, knowledge, feelings— at the disposal of the person in authority over you. This obedience is a humble and intelligent choice. The relationship between a wife and her husband becomes the classroom for learning submission to the will of God Himself.

When my bedside clock sounds an alarm to awaken me in the morning, I *obey* and wake up. I arise and go about my daily tasks because I want to do so in order to maintain orderliness in my life. But I cannot honestly call this acquiescence submission on my part because often my spirit is unwilling! I don't want to get up! However, that same clock tells me when it is time to go to bed at night. No alarm needs to be sounded. In silence I gladly *submit* to the message it delivers!

Submission is not the result of physical weakness but rather the outpouring of spiritual strength. Submission to your husband's leadership is not about *losing* personal rights. After all, in the New Testament, Jesus is not calling for rights for Himself or anyone else. Quite the contrary, He is talking about losing your own life in order to make the greatest gains. The goal is *gaining God-control* in your life. That means *losing self-control.* Yes, I do have rights; and because they are my own personal rights, I *can* and I *do* choose to give them up!

A wife then is not concerned with personal assertiveness, but she is driven to selfless service. She is not obsessed with selfish ambition but absorbed in humble giving. The apostle Peter describes her attitude as marked by a "gentle and quiet spirit."[62] Her manner is pleasant and mild, and she moves through her household in gentle cooperation with her husband and his decisions. She is also calm and quiet, enduring the outbursts and disturbances of others with serenity and without irritation.

HOTEL OR HAVEN

"Feeling at home" enables you to create a spirit that nourishes you and your family physically, intellectually, emotionally, and spiritually. Expressing your own uniqueness as a family ought to be a high priority, and it ought to overshadow all you do to make your home a shelter for your household. If your home is not a reflection of you, if your husband and children do not have a space that represents their own uniqueness, you have work to do lest you become *homeless* in your own home!

Every woman becomes an artist as she makes her house a home for her family. The house and garden become the canvas on which she can unleash her own unique creativity with whatever brush she chooses. You don't have to sacrifice comfort for style. You can choose art and accessories that express who you are and what you like. You can create a distinctive environment in your own small world.

Houses should give sanctuary as well as shelter; they should comfort as well as contain. Bigger houses and more rooms are worthless if that means living rooms in which you dare not live and dining rooms in which the family does not dine and even family rooms in which the family does not have time to gather. When your house becomes a home, the physical and emotional and spiritual needs of your family will be the priority. Your quality of life is not dependent upon quantity of space. *You place importance on spending time together as a family when you plan how to do it!*

The poet-philosopher Edgar Guest once said, "It takes a heap of livin' / To make a house a home." The home, once the center of life and activity, has become a mere filling station for grabbing something to eat or catching a few winks of sleep or even unloading some of your frustrations on the people you are supposed to love the most!

Have you ever stopped to think that your family heritage, as well as who you are and what you will be in the future, becomes readily evident to people who visit your home? They don't have to know you personally or have a conversation with you to learn about your values. They may look at the books on your shelves, the magazines on your coffee table, what you have in your refrigerator; listen to your conversation among yourselves and observe your friends; and see how you have furnished your home and watching your interaction with members of the household.

Nothing calms my spirit or rests my body like being in the oasis that comes from a clean and orderly household. Even though the square footage of American homes has increased by 39 percent, housework has greatly waned. Some reject the option to do housework even when they have the time available. It just doesn't seem important. Although housework has been made easier by technology, it is still a formidable challenge. Cooking meals, cleaning up dishes, household maintenance, laundry and ironing, outdoor chores, repairs, garden and animal care, financial planning and accounting—all are involved in running a home.

These tasks are no longer delegated to household helpers. They are now more often done by computers or equipment, or they simply fall by the wayside. Even cooking is no longer done in the home kitchen. Grocery markets now have departments to handle this task. You stop on the way home from work and select an assortment of entrées for your family members, drive into your garage, unload the meals directly to the table, eat whenever you like, dump the remains in the trash. Meal planning, preparation, service, and cleanup—all are conceivably done within little more than an hour's time, and you saved yourself a lot of aggravation.

People don't like to do what they consider to be dull, boring jobs! Yet some women still find nothing more challenging to their creativity than making their homes a haven for their families. I have hundreds of books dedicated to home maintenance, food preparation, interior design, household organization, and time management. Back in the sixties, even before such books were popular, I found myself gravitating to volumes that would help me be a better homemaker because this was and is and forever will be my passion. I am continually trying to streamline cleaning and improve routine maintenance.

HOLD THE BOUNDARIES

Marriage has undergone a considerable overhaul in an effort to make it more palatable to new worldviews. Couples are too quick to apply permanent solutions (such as, dissolution of the marriage) to temporary problems (such as, the ups and downs typical of all interpersonal relationships). You swallow a pill for a bad headache; you take a pepto tablet for an upset stomach. Is divorce really what you need for a bad marriage?! Couples should rather devote themselves to a permanent and exclusive union that addresses contemporary challenges with creative and appropriate solutions.

In the biblical creation narrative, God's boundaries for marriage are set out clearly. In the Hebrew *Torah* the man and woman are created and then united by God Himself.[63] The New Testament reaffirms these same boundaries.[64] There is complete consistency without any contradiction.

This biblical formula contains three parts. First, leaving father and mother refers to the movement of the couple beyond former ties (the flesh-and-blood, birth relationship with father and mother). The parents who have given you life and selflessly nurtured you to adulthood are not to be cast aside or forgotten. A baby is linked to his mother with an umbilical cord that serves as the lifeline throughout the baby's sojourn in the womb. However, when the baby is delivered, the cord must be cut—not because the baby no longer needs his mother but because the baby now has a new relationship to his mother. The mother is still a *lifeline* but in a different way. She is to feed and nurture the baby; she is to comfort the infant and oversee his care. Their bonding should continue as their lives are uniquely intertwined. In the same way, a husband and wife are to establish a new *first* loyalty to each other in the monogamous union of one man and one woman. Their parents should remain an important part of their lives. They are to be honored and respected. They deserve an investment of time and fellowship, but they no longer have the first place.

Second, the husband and wife are to cling to each other. There is to be an exclusive fellowship between the husband and wife. They are to focus on each other—sharing dreams and goals and nurturing a companionship. Their love for each other is to increase while their covenant commitment to each other remains as the strong and immovable foundation. In the same way that plants require water and fertilizer to grow and flourish, couples must realize that *growing* a marriage doesn't just happen. It demands an investment of time and effort—not for a week or month or year but for a lifetime.

Our children are adults on their own now, but we still have the demands of ministry. Since ours has been a lifestyle ministry that invades the whole of life, we still work at finding times to be alone and uninterrupted. It does not happen easily at Magnolia Hill, but we take a day or two in the midst of our travel schedule throughout the year. Occasionally we set aside time to spend in a remote place. We don't dress for dinner; we don't plan excursions and entertainment; we just enjoy one another in a quiet and peaceful setting. I recommend the getaway from work and even children in order to concentrate on nourishing your marriage and cherishing your spouse.

Finally, the biblical plan calls for a "one flesh" relationship. The Creator's special gift of physical intimacy is God's seal on the marriage. God created the woman from the man and presented her to the man. The two God made out of one are again united to become one. Such a high and holy intimacy is not designed for seeking personal gratification. Married couples actually report more frequent sexual activity and higher levels of sexual satisfaction than couples engaged in sexual activity outside of marriage. Exclusive commitment gives them the edge.

A more stable and enduring relationship creates the environment in which ultimate expressions of love flow naturally. Both husband and wife are to meet the needs of the other instead of their own. This physical intimacy provides the channel for the next generation, but its purpose goes beyond procreation. Rather, it is a means of meeting mutual needs for ultimate knowledge about each other, for uniquely satisfying comfort, for personal relaxation and play, and for mutual resistance to temptation. In fact, a husband is commanded to find satisfaction and joy in his wife, and he is admonished to find ways to meet her personal needs.[65] A wife, on the other hand, is to be available, to prepare and plan for times of intimacy, and to be sensitive to the unique needs of her husband.[66]

Such an intimate relationship provides the exclusive union into which others dare not intrude. Physical nakedness holds no shame for a husband and wife. In fact, total transparency and openness in every aspect of life is to characterize this highest level of intimacy.

To honor God's plan immediately recognizes some protective boundaries:

- exclusive monogamy,
- nurturing fellowship and loyal love,
- physical affection and warm intimacy.

These boundaries protect the marriage from outsiders who attempt to intrude and steal away affections and loyalties. They also wrap the couple in a tender cocoon of loving affection for each other so that the needs of each will be met by the other.[67] Finally, the protective seal of ultimate physical intimacy is an exclusive union in which no one else shares. It is a language of love that does not require words.

FINISH THE RACE

There is a peculiar kind of pride that seems to possess each generation. It is forever obsessed with its own latest fads and ideas. Unmoved and unimpressed with the test of time, those who reject anything the past has to offer are looking for something new under the sun to which they can commit their minds and energies. However, some things never change. The truths recorded in the Bible will stand forever as the standard by which men and women created by God in His image ought to live. King Solomon, a Jew, warned, "Do not remove the ancient landmark."[68] Whether in learning how best to make a marriage work or how to train your child, the closer you come to following the instructions of the Creator, the more successful you will be.

The diamond is a greatly admired and treasured gemstone. Known for its sparking rays, its name (derived from an ancient Greek word *adamandetos,* meaning "iron-bound," from which comes the English word *adamant)* reflects the idea of durability. Without the fortitude to endure throughout the cutting and polishing process, the diamond would never send its sparkling rays! The family is to endure as a diamond, undergoing the constant friction of the chiseling and cutting and polishing that goes along with everyday living so that its members can be enhanced by reflecting the beauty that comes from *family processing!*

1. Gen. 2:15–17; Deut. 6; 1 Cor. 11:3; 14:35; Eph. 6:4.
2. Eph. 5:15–33; Col. 3:19.
3. Gen. 2:15; 1 Tim. 5:8.
4. Gen. 2:15.
5. Eph. 5:18–33; Col. 3:18; 1 Pet. 3:1–6.
6. Gen. 2:18; Prov. 31:10–31.
7. Titus 2:3–5.
8. Deut. 5:16; Eph. 6:1–3; Col. 3:20; 1 Tim. 5:4.
9. Gen. 1:26–27.
10. Gen. 2:24; see also Matt. 19:5; Eph. 5:31.
11. Gen. 2:18–23; Eccl. 4:9–12.
12. 1 Cor. 7:3–5; Heb. 13:4.
13. Gen. 1:28; Ps. 127; 128.
14. Deut. 6:4–25; Ps. 68:6.
15. Eph. 5:18–33.
16. Gen. 2:24.
17. Matt. 19:5; Eph. 5:31.
18. Deut. 24:5.
19. Gen. 2:8–25.
20. Gen. 2:24–25.
21. Matt. 19:1–9.
22. 1 Cor. 6:9–11; see also Lev. 8:22–23; 20:13; Rom. 1:24–27.
23. Prov. 1:7; Rom. 12:1–2; 1 Cor. 13.
24. Hebrew, meaning literally "her writing."
25. Exod. 21:10; Lev. 18–21; Deut. 24:5.
26. Dorothy Kelley Patterson, "The Ketubah" in *The Woman's Study Bible* (Nashville: Thomas Nelson Publishers, Inc., 1995).
27. David Popenoe and Barbara Dafoe Whitehead, "The State of Our Unions: The Social Health of Marriage in America," The National Marriage Project, Rutgers University, 1999, 2–3.
28. Judith Wallerstein, *Second Chances: Men, Women and Children a Decade after Divorce* (New York: Basic Books, 1993).
29. Mal. 2:16; Matt. 19:4–6.
30. Deut. 24:1–5.
31. Matt. 19:4–6.
32. Gen. 2:24; Matt. 5:31–32; 19:3–9; Mark 10:6–12; Luke 16:18; Rom. 7:1–3; 1 Cor. 7:1–16.
33. Mal. 2:16.
34. 1 Pet. 3:1–2, 7.
35. Eph. 5:25.
36. Gen. 2:15–17; see also Num. 1:2–3, 17–19.
37. Eph. 5:21–22, 33; 1 Pet. 3:1–4.
38. Luke 22:26; Heb. 13:17; see also Eph. 5:23–27; Phil. 2:5–8.
39. Gal. 3:28; 1 Pet. 3:7.

40. Eph. 5:25–29; 1 Pet. 3:7.

41. Eph. 5:25–29.

42. Greek, *agapao*.

43. Eph. 5:25–29.

44. 1 Pet. 3:7.

45. 1 Pet. 3:7.

46. Gen. 2:18.

47. 1 Pet. 3:4.

48. 1 Pet. 3:1–6; Titus 2:3–5.

49. *The Washington Times,* 28 January 1999.

50. Karen S. Peterson, "Working Wives Have Ill Effect on Husbands," *USA Today,* 17 August 2000.

51. Gen. 1:28; 2:18; Exod. 18:4; Deut. 33:7.

52. Hebrew *'ezer.*

53. Hebrew *kenegdo* occurs only in verses 18 and 20 of Genesis 2 in the entire Old Testament.

54. Gen. 1:27.

55. Eph. 5:21–24.

56. Greek *hupotasso,* meaning "line up under" or even "place yourself under."

57. Gen. 12:10–20. Note name spellings in this text: *Abram* for Abraham; *Sarai* for Sarah.

58. Gen. 12:10–20.

59. Gen. 20:1–18.

60. Gen. 25:23.

61. Gen. 27:1–28:5.

62. 1 Pet. 3:4.

63. Gen. 2:24.

64. Matt. 19:4–5; Mark 10:6–9; Eph. 5:31. Interestingly these references include the words of Jesus, the influence of Peter on John Mark (the author of the Gospel of Mark), and the teaching of Paul, the greatest apostle.

65. Prov. 5:19; Eccl. 9:9. See also Deut. 24:5; 1 Pet. 3:7.

66. 1 Cor. 7:3–5; Song of Sol. 4:9, 16; 5:2. See also Gen. 24:67.

67. 1 Cor. 7:3–5.

68. Prov. 23:10.

3

Parent or Pal?

REARING CHILDREN HAS NEVER BEEN MORE COSTLY in time
and money than it is in this generation. A *USA Today* snapshot
revealed that an average middle-income family would spend
$160,140 to rear a child born in 1999. This amount includes
housing, food, health care, transportation, clothing, child care,
and education until age seventeen.[1]

Most parents are tied to their children by flesh and blood,
and all have the opportunity to invest tears and years! Yet
Americans seem less willing than ever before to invest their
time, energies, and economic resources in family life. The
family has been replaced in today's culture with individualism
and self-fulfillment. Parents want to be free to live their own
dreams, even if it means spending less time with their children. Nor do children feel any obligation to parents despite
what their parents have done for them. This reduced commitment between parents and children has taken its toll.

Fifty years ago problems in American public schools were
chewing gum, making noise, running in the halls, cutting in
line, and talking during class. Today schools face drug and
alcohol abuse, pregnancy, suicide, robbery, rape, assault, and
even murder. Such spurning of values is no surprise when a
society's people allow disloyalty through adultery; lack of
commitment with easy divorce; rights over responsibilities in
frivolous lawsuits; and blind pursuit of lustful whims in

53

rampant pornography, violent video games, music, and movies featuring sexual fantasies.

Parents ought to take responsibility for what they do not know about their kids and for what they do not do to supervise them—not just for what their children do. Honoring God and His law is the best deterrent to lawlessness with kids and adults. We dare not leave our children in a spiritual vacuum.

Cassie Bernall's mother describes the intuition that overrode her usual respect for her teenage daughter's privacy when she began reading letters with explicit profanity and sexual innuendoes. All-out war broke out. The Bernalls removed Cassie from public high school and monitored her activities, disrupting the lives of all the family members. In reaching out to their alienated and hostile daughter with warmth, self-sacrifice, integrity, and unconditional love, the Bernalls pulled their daughter back to themselves, to God, and to a productive life. When she was tragically murdered, they had no regrets for their investment in her life.[2]

A decade ago *Newsweek* magazine began a special feature with the words "The American family does not exist." They went on to explain that families are appearing in many and diverse styles: mothers working while fathers keep house; fathers and mothers both working outside the home; single parents; multiple marriages bringing children together from unrelated backgrounds; childless couples; unmarried couples, with or without children; gay and lesbian parents.[3] Social critic Midge Decter made this observation: "You can call homosexual households 'families,' and you can define 'family' any way you want to, but you can't fool Mother Nature. A family is a mommy and a daddy and their children."[4]

God Himself is the prototype of parenthood, for He created the man and the woman with the capacity to communicate their love to one another and to Him. As His creation, you have the ineradicable stamp of His love. Parents are able to extend the process of creation through procreation. Out of their love for one another they come together to link hands with the Creator to continue the life cycle. They have the opportunity to communicate their love to their children and to nurture them in such a way as to make them channels of this love. Godly parents love their children as God loved them. They see their children as valuable and unique—an opportunity to continue the generations.

In the agrarian economy of the early days of our country, mother and father worked side by side for family income, and both had a part in rearing the children. They did not do exactly the same things, nor was there upheaval over how the labor was divided. They had a common purpose to provide a stable and nurturing environment for the family. Each had to put aside personal goals to do what was best for the family.

A common purpose is often missing from modern families. Specific, short-term goals are the pathway to more important goals. A common mission statement enables a family to work together in sync to reach common goals. Harmonizing this diversity may call for flexibility in leisure activities for the family to gather more often. A "harmony of differences" prompts quiet moments of fellowship and conversation within the family.

Home ought to be a place where all family members are allowed to be unequal, where everyone knows everyone else's inequalities. Inequalities make the home work. A household in which family members do only what they like cannot exist for the long haul; nor is every family member able to do everything equally well. Each is equally responsible to help carry the load, but each carries his own responsibility and handles it in his own way according to his own giftedness.

FAMILY-TIME FAMINE

Interference from outside forces increases every day. In the early twentieth century, parents were told to keep a rigid schedule with their babies—even scheduling the elimination process! Spontaneous love and attention were forbidden. Dr. Spock swung the pendulum back to gearing the family schedule according to the baby's whim, and discipline was swept under the carpet. Now psychiatrists blame every kid's problem on parents and prescribe stimulant prescriptions for a quick fix even to daydreaming.

The family has been invaded by television, peer pressure, schools, demands from the workplace, the government, and even family experts themselves. Children's loyalties are drawn from their parents to alien surrogates coming from outside the home. These invaders ignore the overwhelming evidence that family breakdown fuels poverty, crime, and general hopelessness in society. Society seems content to leave children to their own devices or consign them to the whim of circumstances whether by abandonment or neglect. A USA Today snapshot illustrated the amount of time adults spend with their children between the ages of six and seventeen during an average week of the school year: 12 percent spent less than twelve hours; 28 percent spent twelve to twenty-four hours; 33 percent spent twenty-four to forty-eight hours; 27 percent spent more than forty-eight hours.[5]

Every parent has not abdicated his responsibility; some are being forced to give up ground by forces they cannot control or identify. The growth of social services, health care, and public education has robbed parents of their traditional roles as nurturers, caregivers, teachers, and job trainers of their own children. There is no place of trust, no foundation of love and learning, no intimate space to provide a long-term, permanent, and secure attachment from which children can go out with confidence into a complex and frightening world.

The "experts" are suggesting that parents aren't competent to make decisions for their own children. Unfortunately some parents are accepting this rejection. Educators are demanding that only the schools can teach skills and instill values. Almost every traditional function of the family is moving from the home to some institution or professional. The elderly go to retirement or custodial care facilities; the sick go to hospitals or clinics or rehabilitation centers; the poor dwell in public housing and are supported with welfare. Ministries to the poor and needy have moved from religious bodies and families to government and for-profit organizations. What was once deviant behavior has now been labeled variant.

Parents have fallen prey to the effort of society to isolate children from adults. Children cannot rear themselves; they need to observe, work with, and even play with others who are older than they. A world without adults is ruled by age-segregated peers and is bereft of standards and examples from those who have gone before.

Parents can also apply the wrong kind of pressures. Unreasonable academic expectations of parents for their children can create an imbalance. Some teens also complain of the "too-muchness" of life—too much to do, too many pressures, too many choices to make, too much to learn. This equals too little free time, too little quality time with parents, too little guidance.

The "frantic family syndrome" fits the hectic lifestyle characteristic of Americans who are obsessed with time-saving technology that fails miserably to deliver what is promised. When traveling overseas, I'm forced to slow down, move at an unhurried pace, sit and wait, enjoy my meal in courses with tea served after dinner.

The frantic American pace shifts child rearing from character development, which takes time and cannot be hurried, to the development of skills, which suggests the more you acquire the better. Seizing an opportune moment without advance planning immediately puts the previously planned schedule on hold or may mean canceling lesser important events. Logic would dictate that character development is primarily the work of parents and usually would take place on the home turf. But to develop skills, third parties are called in, or more likely children are called out to search for more and better skills.

THE NOT-AT-HOME GENERATION

Overscheduling by "hyperparents" means stress for both parents and children. The emphasis on perfection in family life can bring such relentless pressure that children are damaged in the process. Childhood is a time for preparation, not performance. Your child is a masterpiece in progress. Don't expect him to do everything well all the time or to do everything you did or wish you had done. Custom kids are often fashioned through a dangerous cloning process of squeezing them into molds they don't fit.

Even if parents themselves are chauffeuring their children through this hectic schedule, family communication and intimacy are lost in the rush. Today's values seem to be based on what is a benefit to parents in professional pursuits and economic gains rather than on what benefits children. Selfish individualism is inconsistent with strong families and strong communities.

Children need the joy of childhood—a relaxed atmosphere with plenty of time to explore their home setting, to form intimate relationships with their siblings and parents, to learn their family values, and to absorb their family heritage!

Instead, children are living in the backseat of the family automobile as parents hurry them through a plethora of activities. They talk to the backs of their parents' heads as they eat fast food running from one activity to another. They play soccer, do gymnastics, perform ballet, participate in a musical ensemble, do cross-stitch or needlepoint, or belong to a hunting club, but these skills are meaningless if not set in the strength of character and values. A child's "apprenticeship" in a loving family makes the difference.

Parents and children should enjoy each other most in the family setting. Extracurricular activities that disrupt family time should be minimal. Children should not be left without consistent care and supervision. A child is naturally more secure when there is someone to whom he can turn with a problem or sorrow. The parent's presence creates an atmosphere in which your family values and moral principles can be instilled in children. Children who spend most of their time with nonparental caregivers tend to develop the values and lifestyle of the one with whom they are spending the most time.

A YMCA poll revealed that teenagers want more time with their parents.[6] Missing the big events in the life of a child is one of the greatest tragedies in absentee parents. The amount of total contact parents have with their children has dropped 40 percent during the last quarter century.[7] This drop in parent-child contact or even accessibility of the parent to the child eliminates or at least reduces the opportunity for building a strong parent-child relationship and forces the child to look elsewhere for meeting some of his most basic needs. Certainly *quality* time is important, but to offset peer pressures parents need to be prepared to invest a *quantity* of time as well. *There is no quality time without a quantity investment.*

Quantity time will assume its own inherent *quality* performance. You have the opportunity to observe closely the mysterious and unpredictable changes that occur in your children. By being there virtually all the time, you won't miss the milestones of life. As you exercise patience, tolerate frustration, remain flexible, and log time in the parental "waiting room," you are building your own character and laying the foundation for character-building of your children. *In the ordinary events of life, you will experience the extraordinary development of your child! In the midst of mundane routines, you will find the most effective curriculum for life education.*

God wants to create the solitary in the family[8]—an uninterrupted time for parents and children to enjoy, to draw strength, and to find comfort from one another. Take charge of your interruptions. Turn off your cell phone; let the answering machine pick up incoming calls—at least during mealtime.

Making yourself available to help with homework can be valuable personal time with your child. You can monitor what your children are being taught and ascertain if they are learning the essentials.

Phyllis Schafly, an attorney and political activist, has always been first and foremost a mother. She taught each of her children to read at a little desk beside her own.

Children learn to make choices in how they spend their time by observing their parents. I have said no to many leisurely pursuits I would have enjoyed. Ministry demands occupy my discretionary time, and I am not willing to infringe on family time. During my child-rearing years, except in rare circumstances, evenings and weekends belonged to my family. When our children were involved in high school athletics, my husband and I were immersed in their team schedules. When they were in college, we planned family vacations during their break schedules.

Listen to your children when they have something to share—as you travel in the car, during mealtime, in the living room, on the playground! Spend time in silence, just being there, waiting on your child to open up.

Involve yourself with your child—reading aloud from some classic literature, playing a game he wants to play, watching a movie he enjoys. My granddaughter Abigail wants me to watch videos with her. Repetition of the same video suggests that my time was wasted, but the hours spent cuddling my granddaughter as we watch the video is like putting money in an account of love! A child longs to have your presence and attention, even in frivolous pursuits!

How wonderful it is when a child awakens to the voice of mother or father—a happy greeting and cheerful countenance to start the day off! Parents who are at home and available at key times during the day—breakfast, after school, dinner, bedtime—and who share in the activities of their offspring give a decided advantage to building a hedge of protection against many adolescent crises.

My mother entered my room each school morning with an appropriate greeting—"Happy Tuesday morning!" She announced the day of the week. I knew she was happy, and I felt important enough to merit her personal wake-up service. Perhaps even more important than "wake-up service" is "turn-down service." Luxury hotels have it. Tucking your child into bed is a loving touch that gives a child significance and security. I coveted this time with my children and continued it during their teen years. Now they tuck me in when they are home.

My granddaughters are already conscious of how much they enjoy this ritual—goodnight kisses for everyone on the premises, even the dogs! Then Mommy reads a brief verse of Scripture and says a prayer, and Abigail says "pat you," by which she means that she wants her mommy to pat her back as she settles into bed! Rebekah doesn't say much yet, but she already enjoys the ritual, and there are no shortcuts if she is to go happily to sleep!

Parents should read the Bible themselves and encourage their children to read it. A half hour of daily Bible reading will take a child through this library of history, adventure, poetry, romance, philosophy, and theology in less than six months. To biblical wisdom, parents add their own experience, and that requires an investment of time. Children need the primary energies and creativity of their parents!

A parent can establish a heritage of meaningful experiences for a child to learn how to know God. Although direct teaching of biblical truth is essential, never underestimate the power of your example. You can teach only what you know, and you can reproduce only who you are. Listen to their questions and concerns; let them set the agenda for discussion. Spiritual nurture in the home demands your greatest creativity and should include activities that catch the interest and imagination of your children. Taking time yourself to talk about God and pray to God should be a part of your lifestyle. My husband and I have both been fashioned by the prayers of our mothers. We heard them pray for us—even when they were unaware that we were listening.

OFFSPRING OR ORPHANS

The American family has been the victim of a social tidal wave. Families have been left impoverished economically, damaged emotionally, and frustrated socially. The home was established to be the nurturing center with an intimate connection between parents and children—a place to which you long to return rather than accommodations to which you have no ties.

Chief among the scattered debris are children and adolescents who come out of fragmented or dysfunctional homes. The number of mothers employed outside the home has risen. Children need a big chunk of someone's time, energy, and creativity in order to grow and stay healthy and satisfied in the process. After all, an *offspring* is, literally, the child who "springs off" what the parent is. Unfortunately, "country club," "civic club," "career," and even "church" orphans come from families in which parents are so wrapped up in their pet projects that they don't have time to be parents! Children should not be reared on leftover time or energy. Nor should children be turned over to their peers or to contemporary personalities in the entertainment industry to mold their self-concept and character.

In the ancient world, childhood was viewed as merely a prelude to adulthood. The child's value was entirely in the future. Parents today live their lives as if this were true. They are pushing their children into premature adulthood. Toddlers are placed in regimented, daily play school, and they are into "college preparation" before they get out of grade school. Elementary school children are assigned homework that demands hours of their evening time. The leisurely family mealtime is abandoned, and options for recreational or spiritual pursuits are forgotten.

Child labor has taken on new meaning in the academic world. Young children are expected to sit eight hours in the classroom (except for brief recess or a physical education class, which is also regimented and graded, and less than an hour for lunch). Then they bring home another two to six hours of work. Participation in the athletic program demands long hours of practice. The weekends are filled with special projects and term papers.

Cars have become the passage to high school, not college, and certainly not a reward to be bestowed after graduation. This leap is excused because of jobs. Instead of part-time neighborhood employment to which you walked or arrived via public transportation with rescue from Mom in bad weather, young people are seeking adult jobs with benefits in order to get a head start in future employment. They need more money to pay for all their bank card purchases and to keep their personal cars running. Some are virtually supporting themselves. I remember hearing about one family in which the college daughter paid her upper-middle-class parents room and board for sleeping in her own bedroom while attending school, and she also paid for her own meal when the family went out to eat.

In the New Testament, the parents of Jesus carried out their tasks according to the "Law of the Lord" during the days of Jesus' infancy and throughout His childhood and teen years.[9] Even though they may have been aware of the extraordinary assignment embraced by their firstborn Son, they were diligent in their responsibilities to rear Him according to the Jewish law. He received earthly protection from His foster father Joseph and nurture from the breast of His mother Mary. They didn't try to push Him out of the home; rather, they let Him develop and assume His destiny at His own pace. Jesus remained in His hometown of Nazareth for thirty years before He began His ministry or "career."

EARTH OR ETERNITY

The biblical pattern is for parents to receive a child as a gift from God. Aborting a child because of the quality of life he may or may not have or because he may interfere with the lifestyle of the parents is not a viable option for God-fearing potential parents or for single mothers whose own choices have created an inconvenience. Nor should parents feel that they can defer childbearing to a time more convenient for themselves. Their responsibility is to accept the child that God gives and rear him into adulthood, savoring every stage of development. The Hebrews spoke of child rearing as "building sons and daughters." Psalm 128 is still identified as "The Builder's Psalm." Bringing up a child in fear and admonition of the Lord is an awesome responsibility.

Childhood is potentially a wonderful time of unique freedom from cares and abandonment of pressures and the opportunity to enjoy simple pleasures and become acquainted with the beauty of creation. However, during this period of innocence the child is also especially vulnerable to the evil influences in the world. Parents dare not be so concerned about their own affairs that they do not have time or interest to monitor the behavior of their children, nor should they take the road of least resistance to defend them blindly against disciplinary action from other authorities in their lives. Any child who does not learn self-restraint at home will be incapable of exercising self-mastery outside the home.

Parents must be alert to provide an environment of safety and shelter for the slow but steady development of the child from innocence to adulthood. Parents dare not set daunting expectations and apply unreasonable pressures upon their children for academic or social successes as if childhood in itself is unimportant. Parents must make their choices with care as if the child's life depended upon those choices, as it very well may!

Parents ought not to grant a child increasing personal autonomy until moral and spiritual foundations have been carefully lain. The extreme individualism of the modern culture seems to be driving children away from the family hearth and from the life of their local civic and religious communities. In experiencing this untimely separation, children are robbed of the most dependable source of wisdom and safety. They become suspicious of the past, irresponsible in the present, and indifferent to the future.

The rights of children are not the issue. Rather, formation of character and preparation for life must be considered. The best way to learn is still by imitation of what goes before you and by repetition of important truths to be embraced.

Birth rates have fallen precipitously in many countries, including the United States, while divorce rates are surging forward. The acceptance of pre- and extramarital sexuality has become widespread, and cohabitation or living together without the commitment of marriage is becoming commonplace. The trend seems to be toward a decreasing commitment of husbands and wives to one another as well as a declining sense of responsibility on the part of parents to their children.

Regular patterns of contact between children and their adult relatives have become almost nonexistent. Although mothers are home less, fathers have not picked up the slack to compensate for the mother's absence. Even grandparents are too busy to provide times of enrichment. Many children and adolescents spend their lives moving through a variety of out-of-home child care settings, learning in the process "self-care." Only too often taking care of yourself means no care at all!

Latch-key children are definitely a contemporary image. Whether because they live in a single-parent household or because both parents are pursuing careers, these children let themselves into an empty house after school. "Patchwork children" must piece together some coherent identity for themselves out of relationships with parents, child care workers, or even "electronic friends."[10] These children are at risk. Although children must work toward moral independence, parents have a role to play in moving them toward their adult destinies. A day will come when children have been reared and sprout their own wings, leaving home to begin independent living. Then a mother has time to devote a worthy portion of her energies and creativity to her own interests.

Parents must look for ways to meet the physical, mental, emotional, and spiritual needs of their children. They must be certain not to equate the worth of a child with intelligence, accomplishments, or physical appearance. Life is full of ups and downs. Perhaps change itself is the most certain factor in living. It may be difficult now, but something better is coming. It may be wonderful now, but don't be lulled into believing that a challenge is not coming tomorrow.

Families need options planned around their own needs and interests. They need freedom from pressure and uninterrupted, private time for renewal and refreshment away from telephones, drop-in visitors, and prying eyes. They need to be able to set their own pace—to sit and wait or move and go. They need family dialogue to explore the issues of importance to them—world events, contemporary happenings, personal values, lifestyle choices, or philosophical prognostications.

Families also need fantastic celebrations, whether a holiday bash, a family reunion, a private excursion, an ethnic restaurant meal, a vacation to see new places or revisitation to favorite old haunts. Parents can make days special; they can make an environment in which the family can enjoy being together, laughing, talking, sharing thoughts and dreams.

The summer season is especially important because it becomes a bridge between parent and child, leveling the ground between the generations with a more relaxed atmosphere and time to spend together. You can become absorbed in life in ways you cannot do throughout the rest of the year. One family decided to take a "home vacation." They freed themselves from household chores by hiring a maid to clean and a cook to prepare meals. Each family member was allowed to plan a day's activities, including requested menus. They spent a fraction of what they would have spent in traveling to some distant destination, they became acquainted with the attractions in their own area, and they enjoyed the comfort of their own home!

I remember a spring visit to my granddaughters. Rebekah was an infant and Abigail a toddler. Carmen was planting her spring flowers and asked Abigail to help. She dressed Abi appropriately for working in the dirt and equipped her with outdoor gloves, a bucket, and a small shovel. What a busy little girl! Her "help" extended the project for her mother, but Abigail enjoyed doing small tasks. I took photographs for her album of memories. When the flowers bloomed, Abigail pointed proudly to her handiwork.

Summer was travel time in our family. The academic year ended for us just as it did for our children. Most of our travel was associated with my husband's ministry—the annual meeting of the Southern Baptist Convention and a study-tour program or mission assignment overseas. We carved out special times with the children despite our assigned responsibilities. We had meals together; we did not have the distraction of telephone calls and appointments; we did not have the competition of television, movies, or peer interruptions. We shared with our children not only a love for travel but also a compassion for people of the world and an introduction to different cultures and unique ethnic distinctions.

Parents dare not grow weary in well-doing. The foundation for good values starts from birth and includes struggles that don't always seem to be successful or even important at the moment. But they mark the steady path needed to the end result. The Judeo-Christian heritage must be brought to life anew in each generation by women and men whose lives have been transformed by the living God and whose hearts have been filled with holy conviction and strict obedience to the Word of truth from the Lord God.

1. "Cost of Parenthood Rising," *USA Today*, 12–14 May 2000.

2. Misty Bernall, *She Said Yes: The Unlikely Martyrdom of Cassie Bernall* (Spring Valley: Plough Publishing House, 1999).

3. Jerrold K. Footlick, "What Happened to the Family?" *Newsweek*, Winter/Spring 1990, 15–20.

4. Ibid., 18.

5. Cindy Hall and Quin Tian, "Family Time," *USA Today*, 29 August 2000.

6. Kathy Kiely, "Survey: Teens Craving Parental Involvement," *USA Today*, 2 May 2000.

7. John P. Robinson, "Caring for Kids," *American Demographics*, July 1989.

8. Ps. 68:6.

9. Luke 2:39–40.

10. Richard R. Osmer, "The Christian Education of Children in the Protestant Tradition," *Theology Today*, vol. 56, No. 4, 520–21.

4

The Father's Leadership

OUR NATION IS SUFFERING a crisis of fatherlessness. Fathers have moved from the center to the fringe of family life. The Hollywood model for the modern male seems to be marked by irresponsibility.

Men have been removed from their families, and the vacuum is being filled by a process of feminization. Masculinity has been redefined with less importance on effective fatherhood and more emphasis on personal ambition and achievement. Men are less concerned with domestic matters. On the other hand, genuine manliness is not carte blanche for aggressive behavior. It is saturated with virtues that inhibit inappropriate aggression and marked by courage, duty, and even chivalry. Ann Landers said it well, "Too many kids are *mother deaf*. The only thing that will work is *Father Time!*"

Less and less is demanded of fathers, and their role in the family has been devalued and stripped of any authoritative position. That means accompanying social pathologies among its children—delinquency, violence, sexual promiscuity, pregnancy out of wedlock, drug abuse, suicide.

I was surprised to see an article entitled "Father's Primary Influence." Martin Wong began with an admonition to Hong Kong fathers to "devote more time to their families because they have more influence on their adolescent children than mothers." He maintained that children who have a good relationship with their fathers have a "better psychological condition" in terms of self-esteem, self-satisfaction, mental health, life purpose, and lifelong goals. The results clearly showed that the father plays an important part in the child's development. Another survey during the same time frame indicated that 37 percent of the fathers interviewed admitted they had left the rearing of their children to their wives because of their own preoccupation with work. Out of this group, 51 percent said that they spent less than fifteen minutes daily talking with their children.[1]

Strengthening families rests largely on reinvigorating the institution of fatherhood. Even though mothers spend more time with their children, teaching them the lessons of life and training them to be citizens of the world, fathers must be involved in this process as well. Certainly this is true in spiritual matters. Many fathers do want to be more involved with their children.

More than 50 percent of the children born in America will spend at least half of their childhood without a father's participation in their lives. More than one third are living in a household without a father in residence.[2] Fathers tend to play with their children in a different way than do mothers. Few mothers have the strength to lift their children high in the air for a sustained time. Children need this adventurous play and roughhousing just as they need reading and games.

Some have been fooled into believing that fathers were important to boys as a role model and guiding force but unimportant to daughters. However, fathers are equally important to their daughters. Fathers teach girls how to relate to men and how to accomplish their goals in what some describe as a "male-dominated society."

A father helps his daughter develop confidence in herself and in her femininity. He teaches her how to understand male-female bonding, and in many ways he introduces her to the world outside her home. Fathers need to model behavior for a responsible and godly man, and they need to help their daughters know how to identify a godly man when they see one. A caring and loving father will make it much easier for his daughter to have a good feeling about herself and give her the confidence that she is worthy of love and respect.

Recent research indicates that 72 percent of Americans consider fatherlessness as America's most significant family or social problem. A young male is twice as likely to engage in criminal activity if he is reared without a father and three times as likely to do so if he lives in a neighborhood with a majority of single-parent families. Children who live apart from their fathers are five times more likely to be poor than children with both parents in the home. Children who live apart from their fathers are more likely to do poorly in school and even to drop out of school.[3]

Research presents these alarming statistics: 40 percent of the children of divorced parents haven't seen their fathers within the last year; 36 percent don't live with their biological father.[4] A report coming from Japan suggests that Japanese fathers spend an average of seventeen minutes per day with their kids. This statistic prompted a new "father-hood" advertising campaign in Japan to encourage Japanese fathers to share housework and child care.[5]

A father's presence in the home is vital to the rearing of children. Fathers should take advantage of the privilege and duty of sharing in their children's lives. Playing, reading, making things, and going places with their sons and daughters are all important. Sports and recreation are oppressive tasks for me! Fortunately, my husband loves to play. He has been a wonderful playmate for our children. He realizes that play is important to children as a part of their physical, mental, and even spiritual development.

Virtues are learned through playing and having fun. A child develops honesty when making moves on the game board; he acquires courtesies by letting a teammate choose his equipment first; he embraces unselfishness when letting others take the credit; he develops loyalty for his team and fellow athletes; he learns respect for others and their property; he must reach for courage to give his all, even when he is hopelessly behind; he exhibits humility when accepting praise and awards; he develops an attitude of gratitude in acknowledging the contributions of his coach and teammates; and he finds grace when—whether winning or losing—he determines to be a person of dignity so that as a winner he doesn't belittle losers or as a loser he doesn't bad-mouth the winner.

Taking the task of fatherhood seriously costs something. Arriving home exhausted and drained from a day's labor, you have what may be the only time in that day for your children. If you go off to hibernate and relax, you and your family lose. On the other hand, if you rise above your own fatigue and pressures, greet your wife warmly, and interact happily and playfully with your children, they will sense your priorities and your affection for them. Spending time with your family is a gift that money cannot buy!

Children need both parents—emotionally as well as economically. Boys need fathers to learn how to be men, and girls need fathers to learn how to relate to men. In most cases the man a girl first loves is her father. The development of a daughter's relationship to her father, if marked by genuine affection and respect, prepares her to appreciate her femininity and to expect that same affection and respect from other men in her life. Girls who don't have the love of their fathers find it hard to respect themselves and appreciate their

THE FATHER'S LEADERSHIP 75

feminine nature. Fathers need to model responsible manhood for their daughters as well as for their sons. When boyfriends come calling, girls with fathers at home may get a bit more respect from their male callers!

Our daughter has always had a special relationship with her daddy. Even when Carmen was very young, Paige gave her special father-daughter time by taking her out to eat or to the mall. Carmen is married and living in her own home, but she still communicates regularly with her daddy. When Mark asked for Carmen's hand in marriage, Paige went through a lengthy session of questions before committing to give up his precious daughter. The fact that Carmen is a loving and attentive wife, secure in her husband's affections and devoted to being his helper, has a lot to do with the relationship she had with the first man in her life—her own father!

A father can have a private commitment service with his daughter, reminding her of her worth to God as well as to her parents and letting her know that her parents are already praying that God will send her a godly husband. The daughter is asked to promise that she will remain pure in mind and body until her wedding day. Some sign a "Purity Covenant." Others receive from their fathers a gold key ("to her heart") or "purity ring" to be faithfully worn and then presented to her husband when she offers herself to him in purity on her wedding night.

Theodore Roosevelt was a man's man, and yet he was also noted for the impact he had on his four sons. Heroism was truly in their veins; and, as their famous father, the Roosevelt boys were noted for honor and virtue. Roosevelt was completely faithful to his wife, he adored his children, and he was always there when his family needed him. As you would expect, his children spent their lives seeking to live up to their father's example and expectations and working to bring honor to the family name.

What a contrast is found in Franklin Roosevelt, who was also a president of the United States. He was unfaithful to his wife and seemed disinterested in his children. He was not there for his family. His five children recorded nineteen marriages among them, and his own marriage was a sham. Exploitation and corruption haunted his presidency. Even before both parents were dead, the children were getting rich by sharing sordid tales about the dysfunctional family.

Early Christian parents were exhorted by their spiritual leaders to ground their children in Scripture and the requirements for character. This training was not limited to attending classes in religious instruction. Rather, parents were to assume responsibility for supervising their own children in the study of the Bible, telling them the stories of the Bible and drawing moral lessons from those stories. Memorization of Scripture was also encouraged, especially the Psalter, since families could recite or chant psalms together, bringing their personal concerns into a living dialogue with God.

Often religious leaders have been born in direct response to the prayers of devout mothers who, just as Samuel's mother Hannah, promised to return their sons to the Lord. My husband's mother was infertile and prayed a decade before God answered her prayer for a son. She faithfully nurtured him in the Lord and prayed through the years that he would be a committed servant of the Lord. Paige Patterson is a worthy answer to that prayer. He has given his life to preaching the gospel, to equipping men and women for work in kingdom ministries, and to standing for truth whatever the cost.

Chrysostom, one of the fourth-century church fathers, recommended that parents dedicate their children to God just as

Hannah and Elkanah dedicated Samuel. Pastors continue to encourage families to dedicate their children to the Lord. At Central Baptist Church in Decatur, Alabama, Pastor Mark Tolbert invites parents and siblings of babies to join him on the platform. He asks each father to read the "life verse" chosen for the newborn baby. Then the pastor takes the young child, as did Simeon when dedicating Jesus in the ancient Jerusalem Temple, and prays for the child and his parents. Before the congregation, the child is dedicated to the Lord and the parents are challenged to their responsibility of spiritual nurture.

PROVISION, PROTECTION, AND CHARACTER CHISELING

A career and its accompanying economic benefits should never be more important to a father than his children. However, his responsibility in the biblical model is to *provide* the necessities of food, shelter, and clothing for his family.[6] He defeats the value of that provision if he does not take into account his other responsibilities to *protect* (not just physically but also mentally, emotionally, and spiritually) as well as to *lead* the members of his family entrusted to his care.

Fathers must begin early spending time with their babies and toddlers. From the child's earliest memory, a father can watch for openings to pursue significant communication. Small talk will lead to meaningful talk. You have to move beyond your own comfort zone in order to express innermost feelings and thoughts.

Sometimes you need to put your feelings into written words. My husband's "Big Daddy" letters are famous with our children as well as with others who have come under his influence. The addresses are not always pleased with the content of these intimate epistles, but they do know that in the midst of overwhelming responsibilities the letters are written painstakingly in Paige's own hand with much love. And he has always prayed that the messages therein would take root and bear fruit.

Through a monogamous marriage, a husband disciplines his sexuality and extends it into the future through the womb of his wife. His wife enables him to go beyond planting the seed for his children to being intimately involved in rearing them to adulthood and fashioning their characters and lifestyles. A husband gives to his wife the productivity of his labor to support the family instead of spending what he has received for his labor on dissipating and temporary pleasures.

Men are physically stronger and bigger and have the role of protector and provider. They have the assignment of leadership. Women have the functions of gestation and lactation. They become the nurturers of the young. It is indeed a *reciprocal* arrangement with *responsibilities due* and *rewards received* for both the husband and wife.

Fatherless homes have boosted crime rates, lowered educational attainment, and added dramatically to the welfare rolls. When fathers are absent from the home, adolescent boys lack the example of responsible paternity, that is, the model of a dependable provider and the discipline and love of a responsible protector; and they seem to revert to being ruled by their male sexual rhythms. Boys need male role models. Fathers make a unique contribution to their sons and daughters. They generally encourage independence and a sense of adventure.

An IMAX documentary set in Africa showed tremendous destruction of wildlife. The brutal murders of rhinos and other animals were malicious and premeditated. Great effort was expended to find the poachers or predators who would commit such random acts of violence and death.

The investigating team finally discovered that these killings were being done by a group of rogue elephants. As calves who had been sedated and transplanted from their parents and familiar surroundings to a new area, without the supervision of female elephants and the example of the other male elephants, they had followed their own instincts and whims. With their superior strength individually magnified by their gathering as a herd, these elephants were capable of unbelievable destruction.

The game rangers decided to sedate the young bull elephants and transport them back to their original breeding ground and extended families. Amazingly in a short time the elephants were whipped into acceptable behavior. They were not tame enough to approach or ride, but they no longer resorted to the malicious violence that had characterized them when they were left to their own devices.

Children often become their own authorities. They may be reared by surrogate parents such as institutional caregivers, peers, and the entertainment industry. Most violent teens reportedly suffer from a lack of personal and familial structure.

Fathers must be far more than sperm donors! Their role is not limited to the biological contribution they make to the procreative process. Participatory fatherhood is an important ingredient in the rearing of children. Fathers determine half of the genetic makeup of the child, and they usually provide the greater portion of financial resources necessary for the child's sustenance. But as important as these mundane responsibilities is the task of providing emotional resources, beginning with unconditional love. Balance is a critical ingredient in a father's task. Love is balanced with discipline; time alone with a child is balanced with time together with a family; development of mind, body, and spirit must be apportioned appropriately; and time for study, play, and work must all be considered.

Fathers especially are entrusted with spiritual leadership in their families. Nothing gives a better platform than consistent family worship in the home. The Puritans viewed their families as their own "little church." Their home worship included hymns and prayers as well as reading and discussing Scripture.

Fathers ought to make their children feel a sense of worth not only as a valuable member of the earthly family circle but also as a precious part of the heavenly household of faith. They are to instruct their children in righteousness and daily living and train them to follow God's way in all venues of life. They must faithfully rebuke and correct when appropriate. If a father provides this safety net of shelter, security, and adequate life preparation, a child will find freedom and develop in the midst of wholesome and protective boundaries. "Hands-on" fathers can produce "right-on" children!

1. Martin Wong, "Father's Primary Influence," *Sunday Morning Post,* 18 June 2000.

2. "Turning the Corner on Father Absence in Black America," Morehouse Research Institute & Institute for American Values, 1999.

3. Ibid.

4. "The State of Our Union," *SBC Life,* April 2000, 14; from San Diego *Union-Tribune,* 20 June 1999.

5. Mary Jordan and Kevin Sullivan, "Life Without Father—Japanese Version," *International Herald Tribune,* 8–9 May 1999.

6. Gen. 2:15–17; 1 Tim. 5:8.

5

The Mother's Nature Is Nurture

A PASTOR'S WIFE DID A SURVEY among the mothers in her neighborhood: What does your family expect from you? Their answers were amazingly consistent:

- food (specifically, home-cooked meals),
- clean clothes,
- clean and orderly home,
- absence of lengthy telephone conversations,
- cheerful attitude ("no nagging"),
- a loving dad,
- being nice to their friends,
- tucking them into bed,
- attending school activities,
- not assigning chores.

A clear consensus appears. Providing food and clothes and a secure and orderly shelter are at the top of the list before being nice to friends. "Chores" and "nagging" are down the list.

When fifteen hundred schoolchildren were asked, "What do you think makes a happy family?" they did not list money, cars, fine homes, or televisions. They overwhelmingly opted for "doing things together."[1] The earlier you encourage a child to help around the house, the less trouble you will have in persuading the child to do her share in later years. A child's assignment must be based on age, ability, and experience. To overexplain a task with a young child is hard, and to underestimate its importance is easy. Make work fun—put on inspiring music; design a chore chart.

My mother was the heart of my childhood home. She operated behind the scenes, orchestrating the myriad of details required to manage a household of seven. She prepared our meals; she bought, kept in repair, and laundered our clothes; she cleaned the house; she maintained our health program; she supervised our education; she planned our entertainment. I knew that I was loved and cherished because I was worthy of Mother's time and energies. Not snippets of time sandwiched among more important obligations and not leftover time after other work was done—but I, with my siblings, had moment by moment, day by day, year after year of her personal attention—full-time! My mother did have household help, but she was the creative visionary and driving force who assumed responsibility for seeing that everything was done in due course. Her creativity reached every corner of our home and extended to every moment of life. She reared five children from birth to empty nest, and to this day she sends each of us a weekly letter and stays abreast of what we and our families are doing.

One of the most amazing things about my mother's routine was the ease with which she moved, accomplishing all expected of her yet maintaining church activities, club memberships, and her own personal graciousness. With her life consisting of mundane responsibilities and routine activities to keep up with five children born over a decade of time, she must have sometimes despaired that she would ever have time for herself. Staying at home with young children is not an easy task. Yet my mother never complained. Caring for us and making us happy were her chief goals in life. What she encouraged always seemed to proceed from merely pleasant pastime to serious pursuit. She was both a guiding star and a dynamic meteor in our lives. I hope, as we Kelley siblings have our own families, mother is pleased with her products, and she seems to be.

The apostle Paul tells the teachers of women to include in their curriculum instruction on how to be lovers of their husbands and children and home-workers.[2] The Creator God knew our needs and made His assignments accordingly!

From the moment a mother cuddles her newborn child, she is beginning to shape the child's future. The foundation for an understanding of God is laid in infancy. Babies learn spiritual truths through their senses and through their relationships.

Fetuses in the womb are already aware of light and sounds. Studies have shown that children will recognize stories that were read to them while they were in their mother's womb. The most important stage of brain development occurs between birth and age three. Repetition of activities strengthens the child's neurological system, and the repetition of tasks helps a baby retain what he has learned. Every interaction with his parents contributes to the development of the baby's brain. The care and nurture of that child and not career advancement and financial packages must be a mother's top priority!

The potential for giftedness and the kinds of gifts a child possesses appear in early childhood. Creating an educational setting that encourages learning demands some important elements: sensory experiences, choices in the midst of daily activities, exposure to several different languages, reading aloud, field trips, exposure to guests and visitors, opportunities for social interaction that span the generations, repetition and review of tasks and information to be learned. In the midst must be parent involvement with the child and parental hands-on training.

The children of parents who have faithfully prayed for them and invested in their lives from conception have a definite spiritual advantage. Whatever dwells in a mother has the potential to find its way into the heart of her child. Women should be the primary guardians of decency and morality. Moreover, they should inspire men to behave with respect and propriety around women and children.

OPPONENTS OF MOTHERHOOD

Modern ideologies, such as feminism, have convinced many women to give priority to climbing the career ladder unencumbered by husband and children. Many are delaying marriage, homemaking, and motherhood for a more convenient season. Others decide to short-circuit the responsibilities of marriage and indulge in cohabitation with no strings attached. Still others want the security of husband and home as well as the joy of children, but they are determined to have that with a flourishing career.

KEEPING THE HOME FIRES BURNING

Sometimes my involvement with students in higher education seems to teach me far more than I am able to pass on to the students among whom we live and work. I have long been a proponent of the right of mothers to be allowed and even encouraged to give their primary and freshest energies to the home, especially when they need to be nurturing new lives, rearing children, and mentoring adolescents.

Everyone who has pursued higher educational goals knows that if two incomes have been the norm, those school years are lean and difficult. Students fall into the category of "transient" population for most employers. As a student, even if your working hours indicate full-time, your status indicates that one day you will be moving on. If you are part-time, you lose most of the benefits accorded long-term employees—sick days and paid days to refresh yourself, health insurance, retirement. If you are married, your spouse faces the same disadvantage. In these circumstances, even on one income it would seem impossible!

Educational goals may consume at least as much as a decade of your life, and often these years fall when you are establishing your home and beginning your family. My husband and I married during our four-year undergraduate program; we pursued a three-year graduate program in theology; and we eventually spent minimally five years earning postgraduate degrees.

The question is whether anyone gets through these lean years without a family commitment to the task. That commitment is *economic* in the sense of underwriting financial needs to maintain a household; *emotional* in the sense of patient encouragement along a grueling and difficult journey; *mental* in the sense of mind-boggling challenges to expand knowledge and then discern how to use that knowledge; and, for Paige and me, *spiritual* because we believe God had placed these educational goals in our lives to prepare us to serve Him.

Susannah Wesley is one of the most prominent mothers in history. Her fame doesn't come from the identity of her offspring John and Charles Wesley so much as from the fruit of her own pen. She wrote an especially helpful manual including these principles for child rearing.

1. Children need a regular routine in daily life.
2. A one-year-old child can be taught to fear the rod and cry softly.
3. No drinking or eating between meals should be allowed.

4. A mother must first conquer the will in order to fashion the minds of her children.

5. As soon as they could speak, children should be taught the Lord's Prayer to say when getting up and at bedtime.

6. Children must learn early to distinguish the Sabbath or Lord's Day from other days of the week.

7. Children can be taught early to be still during family prayers.

8. Children can be taught early to ask politely for what they want; they should be given nothing for which they cry.

9. Taking God's name in vain was never tolerated; brothers and sisters were to be called only by their proper names.

10. No loud playing or talking would be allowed.

11. A child should take seriously his six hours of school daily.

12. Children sang psalms morning and evening.

13. A child found guilty of wrong doing should not be beaten if he confessed to his wrong and promised to amend.

14. No sinful act such as lying, pilfering, disobedience, or quarreling should be permitted to pass unpunished.

15. A child should not be punished twice for the same act of disobedience.

16. Acts of obedience ought to be rewarded frequently.

17. In anything done to please, though the performance may not be well, the child should be tenderly directed how to do better.

18. A child must be taught rights of property, belonging to self and others.

19. A child must be taught that promises are to be strictly observed.
20. No girl should be taught to work until she could read well.[3]

Although I would not agree with every principle in this comprehensive list (for example, morning and afternoon snacks as well as generous allotments of water throughout the day seem vital to the health of all family members), most of her other guidelines for rearing children are based upon biblical principles rather than sectarian, culture-bound, or gender-limiting notions. Parents would do well to adopt similar guidelines for rearing their children.

Materialism has been a magnet to draw mothers as well as fathers into the marketplace. No longer does the community give legal protection to the mother-child unit, nor does the family itself recognize the importance of this bond by ensuring that adequate economic resources are available from the "family wage."

As income levels rise with the addition of a second income, the bonds of interdependence that once tied people together in families begin to weaken. Women can support themselves and provide for their children without husbands. Employed mothers often leave their children in the care of strangers (usually private institutions but open to whomever would pay the fees and presided over by whomever will settle for the lowest wages on the job ladder). Parental obligations shared by mothers and fathers may be idealistically envisioned, but rarely do they work. The problem of supervision for preschool children as well as for school-age children who arrive home before either parent does remains a matter of particular concern.

MAINTENANCE OR MOTHERHOOD?

Being a mother is a divinely appointed ministry. Motherhood is not to be fit around a professional career and other personal pursuits. A mother ought to provide solace and comfort for her household. She has the sensitivities to feel what they feel, and they know she loves and cherishes them. She should be the "distribution point" for the lovingkindness and mercies of God.

God portrays Himself in Scripture as Father, but He also compares His love for His creation with the love of a mother because He wants to emphasize the depth of His tenderness and breadth of His loyal love.[4] Especially is this tender love important to the infant and young child as a secure foundation for his future. Yet you should never underestimate the imprint a mother can make on her child and the value of that influence even when the child enters adulthood. The sense of a mother's love and care remains. My mother continues her influence on me, and I'm more than half a century old! She prays for me every day; she writes newsy letters to me every week; we talk on the telephone throughout the week; she follows all that I do in my home and ministry.

Full-time mothering is not without its challenges. For example, you can experience loneliness and isolation even when you are in the midst of a "crowd" of children. You often feel cut off from the outside world, and you lose some of the friends you had "B.C." (before children). You may feel the absence of professional status robs you of personal identity. When old friends abandon you, when you no longer have tangible evidence of your accomplishments, when your wardrobe goes to pot and you can't seem to get your makeup on in the morning (nor does there seem to be any need to look attractive), you begin to doubt your value as a person and lose sight of your contribution to life. You feel out of control of your own life. You are working harder than you've ever worked and have less to show for it.

Mundane household tasks or the desire to have unlimited recreational time did not draw you home, but rather your personal passion for loving, caring for, and training your children did. Every mother needs to build a support system of family and friends, including some women who are stay-at-home moms. You have to learn your job. Yes, it is a job—a very challenging one! You will make mistakes, and you will need the wisdom and counsel of those who have gone before.

When you get discouraged about your lack of productivity, make a list of all that you did in a day and acknowledge your accomplishment of all the tasks that are a part of caring for children. You should keep your mind active with reading and perhaps even professional updating. During the almost twenty years I spent nurturing children and teens, as a theologian I grabbed a few minutes to translate a passage from the Greek New Testament or the Hebrew Old Testament. I accepted an assignment to prepare an article or chapter. I read widely and filed articles of significance. I discussed theological issues with my husband.

Parenting is a full-time profession and should be honored not only by those doing it but by those looking on as well. How strange that taking care of someone else's children is considered a legitimate professional pursuit; whereas to choose to care for your own children is thought to be irresponsible and unwise. A parent's task of bonding with her child is done minute by minute, hour after hour, day to day from year to year. Set in the cement of unconditional love and unrequited care, such an awesome task cannot be done in a minute here and an hour there, but it is all-consuming of time, energy, and creativity.

Augustine, perhaps the greatest of the ancient early church fathers, living A.D. 354 to 430, often spoke lovingly and reverently of his mother Monica. The prayers and godly lifestyle of this humble North African homemaker were used of God to bring Augustine to salvation, to prepare him for kingdom service, and to undergird him in his outstanding ministry, which continues even today.

In her youth the simple and untrained Monica developed an intimate relationship with God. She had a remarkable ministry of intercession, praying for her unbelieving husband Patricius, a pagan man guilty of adultery, drunkenness, and violent fits of anger. Monica could not change her husband's heart or the way he lived. She could not protect her son from the negative influence of his father. However, she did what she could in training Augustine in the things of the Lord and taking him to God's house for spiritual training. She also loved him unconditionally and unselfishly. Augustine once commented that no honor he could give to his mother could be compared to "her slavery" for him!

Although Augustine followed his father's example in his early adult years, he must have cherished his mother's faith. He was aware of her tears, which he described as watering the earth wherever she prayed! God also has a word about tears: "They that sow in tears shall reap in joy."[5] Monica was faithful in praying, living her own life with godly consistency and continuing a deep and unchanging love for her son. Although God seemed to ignore her petitions, eventually He gloriously brought Augustine to Himself! Augustine later testified that his father was unable to overcome the piety of his mother who became the ultimate influence on his own young life.

A mother's tears surely must move the hearts of their children and even the heart of God Himself. The psalmist writes,

"You put my tears into Your bottle. Are they not in Your book."[6] I still cry over my children. I feel their hurts; I sense their disappointments; I dream their dreams; I miss their fellowship.

Every mother needs a tear jar. She begins by filling it with her own tears of frustration, suffering, and even joy. When my granddaughters are in the midst of a sorrowful cry, I can reach for an ordinary canning jar labeled appropriately. There is something very distracting for a wailing child when you are encouraging her to keep crying so that you can fill up the tear jar. Such sweet tenderness will undoubtedly stop the tears as the child forgets her sorrows and happily returns to her task.

Rearing a child brings the whole range of emotion. You may go through the mother of all storms, but God-fearing mothers have available "the God of all comfort."[7] God controls the final outcome of what He has allowed. He reveals to you only what you need to know about the storms.

Motherhood is indeed a mission from God, a task unsurpassed in importance. A mother's earthly work is constantly under the shadow of eternal consequences. The Lord Himself challenges mothers to immerse themselves in the task of rearing up godly children through teaching them God's Word and praying for them and *never, never* giving up on them. Thousands of mothers gather in cities around the country through the Moms-in-Touch program to pray for their children, their children's teachers, the school principals, and the local boards of education. These mothers don't offer brief, generic prayers. They do serious and specific intercession for their children and for those who are in positions to influence them. These women are a formidable force in the courts of heaven! Nurturing the young hearts and molding the innocent minds is the first step in training up a generation to impact the world.

A mother experiences the iron grip of a newborn around her finger! That baby simultaneously feels security and confidence in the one to whom he clings so tenaciously. The "God-shaped vacuum" in every child makes his heart pliable. That vacuum is not filled by instinctive faith, and parents have a God-given responsibility to introduce their children to God by revealing to them who He is in carefully planned ways.

One of the most neglected tools for family unity is the celebration of the Lord's Day. This special day is not merely a day of rest from your work for pursuing your favorite entertainment. Contrasted to the pull of the allurements of the world should be devotion to the Lord and appropriate piety honoring Him in worship and praise. The family needs privacy, tranquility, and even seclusion from the rest of the world in order to worship, relax, and enjoy fellowship together.

The weekly Sabbath is greatly loved and cherished by the Jews. They anticipate its coming and then look back upon its memories. The house is cleaned; the table is set with the best china, glassware, linens, and candlesticks. A special meal is prepared in advance since no cooking can be done on the Sabbath itself. The day begins at sundown and is formally welcomed by the family dressed in their finest clothing, the mother's lighting of the candles, the recitation of prayers, the reciting of Proverbs 31:10–31 by the father or a child in honor of the mother, and then a festive family meal.

Observance of the Lord's Day by Christians should focus on delightful spontaneity rather than worrisome constraints. Wearing special clothing, eating favorite foods, enjoying unique family rituals, indulging in extra relaxation and rest, and perhaps playing with special toys should be tempered with a slower pace. Sunday should be the best day of the family's week!

When our children were young, we traveled with my husband to his itinerant preaching assignments. However, when the children needed to be a part of our home church activities, I remained with them. We began "Sunday lunch" for our extended family. Preparing meals and even cleaning up were never drudgery for me as I reflected on our family fellowship.

My husband and I now observe the Lord's Day in a different setting week by week, but we relax in our hotel room on Sunday afternoon—napping, reading, and having a cup of tea. When my grandchildren are with us on Sunday, I pull out their "Sunday Boxes," in which are some special toys and activities for quiet play. Opened only on Sundays, its treats can be anticipated and associated with the Lord's Day. Abi and Beka are delighted with this Sunday tradition.

Mothers need time to renew their energies, revive their spirits, and revitalize their bodies:

- Daily diversions—an hour to spend in spiritual meditation or quiet relaxation without interruption.
- Weekly withdrawal—a trip to the beauty salon or a neighborhood Bible study.
- Annual abandonment—getting away for several days or even a week to evaluate the past year, look at current happenings, project future goals and plans, or enjoy something for sheer pleasure and joy!

WHAT'S A MOTHER TO DO?

Training a child in earthly or heavenly wisdom is a task that must continue throughout life. It is done with transmitting facts and general knowledge and holding up a standard—the virtues of godliness; it is accentuated by the influence of others; it is enhanced by inspiration through words of encouragement and sharing of examples; it is prodded along by holding out appropriate inducements that would catch the imagination of the child; most of all it is imbedded in the child's heart and mind by lifestyle teaching from one who emulates what is taught in daily interaction with the child. No one is equipped to do the job as well as the mother.

Children learn by observing situations and understanding the rationale for responding to those situations. Although many people see "right and wrong" as relative and subjective, ignoring any absolute standards outlined by God, only God can give a moral sense of right and wrong that doesn't change or disappear with the times. A child's moral and spiritual well-being demands the same careful and purposeful attention you give to their physical and educational well-being. The spiritual foundation becomes the bedrock for character formation, decision making, and the pursuit of life's work.

Reading is the basis for learning; it motivates and enriches the learning experience. Children are not born loving to read; this desire must be cultivated. George and Barbara Bush have a special love for reading. Their grandchildren are invited to awaken them by climbing into their bed, together with the dogs, to enjoy a great time together reading. Children's books are kept on a shelf in the bedroom, and each child can make a selection for reading. No outside interruptions are allowed. What a cozy experience to hold a child in your arms or on your lap in an intimate setting and offer your undivided attention!

When our children were young, my husband and I put a bounty of one hundred dollars on certain books we wanted the children to read![8] Although we could have forced them to read the volumes without monetary reward, we wanted them to read with purpose and be prepared to discuss the books.

In the home every child should have a bookshelf or some surface for his own print materials—in the kitchen, by the beds, near the toys, in the bathroom, and definitely near the television. I have purchased facsimiles of characters from the books and videos Abi and Beka love. I look for bound books about the video stories they enjoy. I don't want them to settle for only television and video as they are introduced to the great classics in literature.

Mother is in a position to help the child gain a measure of control from infancy. Instead of letting a child's body and desires control him, a mother can train the child's heart and mind to be the governor of his behavior. To prepare a child for productive life is no small task.

Some parents are enslaved to their own children, responding to the child's whims or leaving the child to do or not do anything according to his own desires. That is sad for those victimized by a child out of control but even more tragic for a child who is void of a rudder to give him guidance in what he should do and when he should do it. To see a child running along the beach laughing is delightful. Boisterous running in the aisle of an airplane by the same child is obnoxious and dangerous for himself and others. A child's tears over the loss of a pet touch your heart. But for the same child to cry and whine because the pet will not do as he commands is selfish and cruel for the pet and the child. To enjoy a child's delightful chatter in conversation is a treat, but to endure a child's continued interruption of adult conversation and monopolizing of every gathering is annoying. The wise Solomon reminds his readers in the book of Ecclesiastes that there is a time for everything, and that axiom is true for children as well as adults![9]

Training or nurturing a child is an all-encompassing task that includes shaping, developing, and even controlling the child's personal choices and action; whereas teaching a child simply refers to the task of passing to him knowledge or facts. Teaching causes the child to *know*; it fills the mind with factual knowledge. On the other hand, training causes a child to *do;* it fashions his habits and helps him discern how to use the knowledge he has accumulated.

Since no human being is perfect, each must be fashioned to adopt restraint (that is, to discern between right and wrong) and to accept stretching and remolding (that is, to reach his greatest potential). Although each child has limits beyond which he cannot go, every child deserves to reach his greatest potential.

To train your child, identify his strengths and weaknesses through careful observation and much prayer. The counsel of others will provide more objective observations, but no one is as equipped as the parent to study the child and determine his needs. And no one except the parent has the ultimate responsibility for training the child. What a child needs more than any opportunity or perceived advantage is interaction with his parents. Others will be called upon to enrich and reinforce what the parents are seeking to do, but the responsibility for training the child rests with the parents.[10] To listen to a child's heart and to answer the questions from his mind takes time. Being the mother to young children is usually a short stint, but motherhood is a statute without limitation!

Mothers must show an interest in what their children enjoy doing. I hate athletics; I despise spectator sports; I loathed having my child involved in contact sports. However, my children, as their father, loved all of the above. I could have done something on my own, but I chose to have fun with them.

When my son became involved in team sports—football, basketball, baseball, track—I walked away from ministries to women; I put aside traveling with my husband, shopping, afternoon teas, reading magazines and catalogs, watching old movies. I faithfully followed the team; I equipped my trunk with towels, ice chest, Gatorade, healthy snack foods, as well as backboard and medical emergency kit for the paramedic I hired to attend these events. I fed the team after each game with homemade delicacies. I dressed in school colors, an official team shirt, photo button and ribbons monogrammed with my son's photograph and name. For that season of life, this assignment was my passion demanding all the creativity and energy I could muster. When my daughter played basketball, it was a similar drill. I don't think either of my kids ever performed without at least one parent in the audience!

Don't feel sorry for me. I did not lose my personal identity during these years in which my life revolved around my children. They hold some of my happiest memories. I moved into that season of life as I have all others with a determination to make it special. I had fun! Some of the most unique parties I ever planned, some of the most delectable culinary experiences I ever devised, some of the sweetest and most genuine expressions of gratitude I ever received, and definitely some of the best work I ever did came in this season of my life.

These years gave me abiding satisfaction and no regrets. My kids are awesome! Some of their peers were even deceived into thinking I was a bit awesome! I wouldn't take anything for these memories! The best present I've given my children is my presence in their lives day in and day out!

Another task of every mother is to develop in her daughters a charming manner that draws others—not because of a mere outward veneer but because of an inner spirit of winsome beauty and gracious manners. When my children were young, I always helped them to prepare written notes of appreciation for gifts and special treats. Before they could write, they would draw a picture or enhance a note I wrote in their behalf. They are very conscientious to this day in responding with written words of gratitude to gestures of kindness. Especially do I remember the many calls and notes and remarks that followed the wedding of our daughter Carmen. Many were touched by the personal expressions of gratitude Carmen wrote in her own hand and style and with very specific words about each wedding gift and every event honoring her.

FAMILY MEALTIME

Families who do a good job of communicating tend to make the dinner hour an important part of their day. You don't have to spend hours cooking as if you were trying to impress someone, but you must commit yourself to making delicious and nutritional food. Sometimes the easiest presentations are the most appealing. When an entrée or dessert is good, you don't need bells and whistles to brag. Your family will do that for you!

Family leisure seems to be declining even while the work is being streamlined through technology and the workweek shortened. Employees seem so starved for time that they are eating breakfast in the car on the way to work or at a desk when they arrive. The dwindling focus on family meals and lengthy commutes, as well as greater work demands, is taking its toll. Still there is no better family gathering place than the table at mealtime. All family members have to eat; most like to eat, bringing a certain sense of eagerness and anticipation as well as relaxation to the scene.

Family mealtime, even for my husband and me, is carved out of the chaos and busyness of the campus and of our bustling, public home. If weather permits, Paige and I gravitate to the deck for a peaceful and fragrant oasis in which to enjoy our meals without interruption of telephone or other distractions. We give each other undivided attention. We share the day's events and usually glean information as well as enjoy laughter and relaxation in the process. We spend time together, listen to each other, pray together, read and discuss God's Word, celebrate life and family, provide comfort and praise for each other, and say over and over again in the process "I love you."

The number of women who want to cook is shrinking, and those who do have forgotten that you eat with your eyes first. Yet "family nourishment" has long been recognized as important for the emotional and social development of children. A study from Harvard Medical School has added importance to the family meal, suggesting that children who eat with their parents are healthier than children who are forced or even allowed to prepare their own food. Kids who fend for themselves tend to eat fewer fruits and vegetables, which give them the nutrients they need for normal growth and development. The junk food they choose puts them at risk to develop an unhealthy adult life.[11]

Ground rules are necessary to maximize the value of family dinner time.

- Every family member should be expected to be present.
- No interruptions should be allowed.
- Peaceful relaxation should be encouraged. Reprimands and chastisement should be avoided.
- Meal planning should be a mother's priority—not just for nutrition but for aesthetically pleasing plates, tantalizing scents, and a carefully set table.
- Topics for discussion in which all participate should be chosen.

Mealtime is the proper arena for teaching simple table manners. How tragic it is to see men and women who are well prepared academically and professionally and yet who lack simple table manners—chewing with your mouth closed, not talking with your mouth full, holding your fork correctly, using the proper utensils, knowing when to begin eating or what to do when you finish. Manners are taught by example and by gentle and appropriately timed correction.

Mealtime is the perfect setting for the family to reconnect and thus to express lovingly their importance to one another. If there is a cornerstone in the family, it's probably resting beneath the family dinner table! The atmosphere must be conducive to happiness and joy and to expanding horizons with information for and understanding of one another.

Mealtime invites a slowing down. Whether at your kitchen table, on the porch, in the backyard, or at a neighborhood park, mealtime provides the opportunity for exchanging information, for updating on family news, for discussing world events, for sharing dreams and goals, for help in problem solving. Sometimes the family gathering serves as a clinic for patching up the bumps and bruises received in life and for encouraging and comforting one another. Fun and laughter are generally interspersed, a perfect way to release the tensions of the day. Parents must be prepared to begin the conversation and even move it along if children are withdrawn or timid. They must have something worth discussing, and they themselves must be willing to talk. Parents must also be careful not to confine their conversation to one another, ignoring the children. Each child—even the youngest—must be included as a part of the "table talk." Conversation is one of the most effective learning tools available to a parent.

Nothing can nurture skills in talking and listening like a happy hour around the family table. The process of learning communication skills will have an effective training lab and a wonderful testing ground. The finer points of courteous interchange can be developed in this natural setting. Family members can learn to laugh at themselves and at one another.

Storytelling takes on new importance and can be learned by trial and error before a captive audience.

Families that spend time together on a regular basis will grow closer. The bonding process cannot be done in a marathon weekend or a few years of special attention. Nowhere is the strong sense of family identity any better fashioned and more encouraged than at the dinner hour. Children are given a sense of belonging, and their worth as full-fledged members of a family is apparent. Parents have regular opportunities to hear how their children feel about themselves and about their lives. When children share their own thoughts, ideas, and feelings and find them heard and respected, they learn that what they think and say is important—at least to the family!

Mealtime may be a parent's most productive classroom. Whether in formal family worship or informal talk, there are opportunities to teach eternal truths and establish a foundation for bedrock faith, together with releasing unconditional love, in this very natural flow of a routine family gathering. What better setting to work at building character in the lives of your children. Family values and morality can be encouraged directly and indirectly. Here you have the seedbed for building happy memories that last forever. With very little effort and much commitment, family and food can merge into meaningful mealtimes. Creativity and fun are meshed with faithful planning and serving of food in what is set aside as a family event.

CONCLUSION

Almost a century ago Congress declared the second Sunday in May as Mother's Day. The citation commended mothers who are "doing so much for the home . . . and [for] religion, which leads to good government and humanity." The vast majority of Americans in 1914 believed that full-time mothers had a high calling and that they were performing a task vitally important to all Americans. No institution has been able to provide a substitute for mothers. They have been the indispensable moral backbone of our homes and neighborhoods.

What a different scene we find as the new millennium dawns! Mothers are extolled for bringing home a paycheck and ridiculed for staying at home with their children. The norm for mothers seems to be putting careers on the front burner with children as an afterthought. The trend is delaying childbirth and then turning over care of the child to others in order to keep careers on line.

Affordable institutional care for children continues to be a phantom. In some states, the average cost for day care for a preschooler can be almost twice the annual cost of college tuition, without any real guarantee for a quality program.[12] What would it mean to the tax structure to pull those costs down? How much income would be required for a family to invest what would equal double the planned college tuition for each child?

A series of caregivers is not the same as the undivided and passionate attention of the mother for any child. Studies suggest that the lack of a mother's nurture will result in the loss of brain hardware for a child. Special and abundant eye contact from one person—the child's mother—is important because of the transfer from the mother to the child of creative energy, which is measurable in the eyes, voice, and reactions. In this way mothers actually participate in fashioning the baby's brain. The brain does not perfunctorily grow by a set pattern but through stimulation. The mutual gaze between mother and child gives the child a sense of self, the emotional well-being that causes optimum development, arousing the imprint of the baby's brain. A mother's eyes of love and trust help the baby develop physically, becoming self-aware and self-conscious.

Through mirroring, children read a response in the face of their mothers. They learn what is acceptable or not acceptable and usually modify their behavior accordingly. The mirroring process is the first step in learning how to interact with others. It is much like a computer. A child can read in his mother's eyes, "Download not completed" or even worse "Access denied," and he is adrift, not knowing where else to turn for help and acceptance. Experiences from early childhood have an impact later in life.

In the Chicago Art Gallery is a uniquely insightful portrait of a mother breastfeeding her child by American artist Mary Cassatt. The child's eyes are focused intently on the mother's face rather than the food supply. Among mammals, only babies from the human species are able to look at the mother while nursing. The miracle of design by the Creator through the prominence of the mother's breast and the distance from the infant's nursing position makes it possible for the baby to focus on the mother's face. God knew that this eye contact would be vital for the mental and social development of the infant. This phenomenon is one reason humans are more intelligent than all other species.[13]

Some have suggested that the home, especially as primary child care facility, is the toughest workplace of all. The demands are unrelenting and sometimes unreasonable. A wife/mother is on call twenty-four hours a day. She doesn't get paid a basic wage much less overtime. The work is most often physically, emotionally, and mentally draining, and it can be downright boring. Her work is not recognized, nor is she thanked for her selfless labor. Yet most wives/mothers, as I, struggle on, knowing that this too will pass. Mothers know that it will be over sooner than later. Mothers are natural mentors for their children. A human mother, like a mother bird, will hang onto her child until the child has strengthened "his own wings" in order to fly away on his own.

The American nation is living proof that children need to see more of their mothers and less of the world. No woman should let the world convince her that she has no choice about working in her home instead of the workplace. Every woman has a choice, and she must make that choice according to the needs of her own family and not according to the pressures of her peers. For example, a mother who is single (whether because of divorce or death) may have to enter the marketplace because she is the breadwinner as well as the caregiver.

Mothers who remain in their homes do work, but they are not paid in dollars and cents. Mothers who unselfishly devote themselves to their children deserve special praise. Maybe you have not seen mothering as an important job. You may feel it lacks intellectual stimulation and worthwhile productivity. Think again! Mothering thrives on creativity and energetic activity, and intellectual challenges abound. A true spirit of creativity will always find expression, and one of the best arenas for creativity is nurturing. Mothers shape the lives and futures of their own children.

1. Nick Stinnett and John DeFrain, *Secrets of Strong Families* (Boston: Little Brown & Co., 1985).

2. Titus 2:3–5.

3. Norman V. Williams, *The Christian Home* (Chicago: Moody Press, 1952), 69–73.

4. Isa. 49:15; Hos. 11:3–4; Luke 13:34.

5. Ps. 126:5.

6. Ps. 56:8.

7. 2 Cor. 1:3.

8. What were the books? They included *The Spirit of the Disciplines* by Dallas Willard, *Passion and Purity* by Elisabeth Elliott, and *Peace Child* by Don Richardson.

9. Eccl. 3:1–8.

10. Deut. 6:4–9.

11. "Eating Together," in *Time,* 3 April 2000.

12. "Affordable Child Care Remains Hard to Find," *USA Today,* 9 February 2000.

13. Notes from an address by Christine de Vollmer during the World Congress of Families II, Geneva, Switzerland, November 1999.

6

The Child's Obedience

FOR THIS GENERATION TO DENY YOURSELF anything or to defer gratification is to oppress or enslave. Women have fallen prey to an impatient and selfish mind-set that demands having it all now. They want home, adoring husband, model children; they also want to reach some challenging professional pinnacle before age thirty. Couples want two cars in the garage, a television in every room, color-coordinated furniture and draperies. Unselfishness is missing. Parents don't want to give up things in order to teach their children principles because to do so is inconvenient.

Fidelity to commitments, especially to your own spouse and family, is absent. Because marriage is a commitment, divorce is devastating to children. When marital commitment is shattered, a lot more than a marriage is broken.

Respect for authority has fallen away. Personal liberty surpasses the law and supercedes consideration of others. Breaking the law becomes all right if you know and do what you believe is best for you. Your child may go a lot further than you since your children tend to magnify your weaknesses and not your strengths.

Deficits in character indicate moral lacking, and that produces moral compromise, which will then create immoral young people. Inappropriate surrender to children intent on having their own way does not limit damage; ultimately it increases it. What parents do to their children, their children will do to society. If a parent doesn't prepare his children, society will be less than it ought to be before the next generation takes the reins.

WHAT THE BIBLE SAYS ABOUT CHILDREN

Children have tremendous significance throughout Scripture. In the Old Testament, they are the gift of God.[1] Jews have traditionally rejected abortion and infanticide. Children were considered to be their parents' hope for care in their old age and the means for parents to continue the generations.[2] Jewish parents viewed children as the sign of God's blessing.[3] Infertility or childlessness was considered a curse.[4]

Children were an integral part of the Jewish household. When isolated from adults, children are bereft of standards and support; and adults lose the joys of interaction with youthful vitality. A child learns about himself and develops his skills from observing, playing, and working with adults. Parents and children should plan a maximum and minimum of time and activities within the family setting.

As soon as they were old enough, Jewish children were assigned household chores. They were carefully taught God's Law. All education was tied to holiness, and all of life was the classroom. The real center for educating Jewish children has been the home, and the responsibility for that education belongs to the parent. Before the time of Jesus, children were taught in their homes.

By the New Testament era, a teacher may have been employed by the synagogue to oversee the educational process. Jesus blessed the children who were brought to Him and even used children as a model to illustrate how His followers were to enter the kingdom of heaven.[5]

In the Decalogue, two commandments deal with the issue of authority. God and parents are the primary authorities to help a child develop a consciousness of his obligation to God and others. Children are admonished to hear and obey their parents because such a response represents personal righteousness and thus pleases God.[6] The fifth commandment concerns honor due parents, which opens the way for the child to have a long and blessed life.[7] This commandment is set apart from others by its unique promise, which is restated in the New Testament.[8] Honor is due to other authorities in life, such as kings, judges, priests, and prophets.[9]

GOOD PARENTS WITH "BAD" CHILDREN

Wounded parents—mothers and fathers who did all the right things—have watched painfully and with great sorrow as their children took a wrong path. These children made a deliberate choice to reject the love and training they received from godly parents. Instead they chose to pursue their own ungodly and rebellious agenda.

The prophet Samuel suffered humiliation and heartache. His sons Joel and Abijah were out of his control, and the elders of Israel recognized that these men were not morally fit or spiritually prepared to lead the nation.[10]

Jesus described a father who experienced untold agony of spirit over the younger son who demanded his inheritance early and departed from the familial home to go his own way. He wasted his inheritance on an immoral and decadent lifestyle until he was destitute. Sleepless nights, a broken heart, sorrow and suffering of the worst kind—some parents know exactly what the wounded father felt. The prodigal in this parable returned but without his inheritance, without his health, and having wasted something far more precious than money—days of his life![11]

Where do hurting parents turn? God is the model for fathers and mothers. He had trouble with His chosen children—Israel—not to mention countless men and women in subsequent generations until now! What did He do? He grieved over His rebellious children. He constantly called them back to righteousness and to Himself; but through it all He loved them. God gives you and your children free will. Parents are responsible for training and nurturing their children in the Lord. A consistent and loving influence is vital for directing children in the right way. The home is an incubator in which to dispense wisdom and influence.

Mothers and fathers dare not withhold forgiveness from a rebellious child who returns. Rejection of a broken child is not the response of a godly parent any more than God would reject one of His repentant children. Parents must put aside their rights and be willing to administer unconditional love. The father in Jesus' parable immediately and without hesitation received his wayward son. No questions were asked; no demands were made; the father opened his arms to receive the prodigal. Restoration was immediate and complete.[12]

In Proverbs, the Hebrew word for *son*[13] is not used exclusively of young children. Throughout the Old Testament the word denotes male descendants in genealogies, inhabitants or members of a family, or a nation or men described as "mighty" or "wicked." The appropriate response expected from an adult son would not be the same as from a young child or even a teenager. However, apparently even adult children should listen respectfully to wisdom and insights shared by their parents; and the implication is that they should seek input from mother and father on matters of importance.

INVESTING IN ADULT CHILDREN

My husband and I have been blessed with godly and committed parents. We also had good teachers in school and church, and virtues were still a part of the learning package. At home we heard and saw the life choices and patterns of our parents. We observed them throughout the day, over the weeks, through the months for years and years. Our parents walked what they talked, and the living of their lives made a greater impact on us than what they said. We have never ceased to have a need for their words of wisdom and instruction.

My parents-in-love died years ago, and yet we still think of them when important decisions are to be made. My husband is a scholarly theologian, a gifted interpreter and communicator of Scripture, and a recognized and respected international religious leader; yet he continues to honor my father, a humble layman who has walked with the Lord through the years. He listens intently and respectfully to whatever my father has to say.

RIGHT OR WRONG OR IN BETWEEN

Christians are commanded to do many things that emulate the Christian life. There are also prohibitions. Between what is commanded and what is forbidden are choices to which Scripture does not directly speak. Guidelines for a believer's ethical decisions are summarized in what my husband calls "Corinthian Principles":

1. Will the action cause someone to be hurt or weakened through your influence?[14]
2. Will the action be edifying to you personally?[15]
3. Will the action glorify the Lord?[16] Liberty is not license to do anything but rather a loving commitment to let God's Word be the standard for all decisions.

CHOOSING A LIFE'S PARTNER

Going from one relationship to another has become a national pastime for young people as well as adults. Frivolous relationships plant the seeds for a series of companions with no concern for emotional attachments outside the boundaries God clearly sets for covenant marriage. Parents are often completely excluded from the modern dating system and consequently from the child's process of selecting a life's partner.

The loss of basic distinctions between masculinity and femininity in co-ed relationships is alarming. Your sons may be bombarded by aggressive females who clearly become the initiators throughout a dating relationship. These girls spend their money, or that of their parents, to pursue boys. Even if the boys like to be pursued, this reversal of roles is a tragedy that will forever plague the girls and boys who are a part of its entanglement.

God created men to be initiators and eventually heads of households; He created women to be responders to that leadership and finally helpers in the homes. If this is part of the nature of a man and a woman, then it should begin even in earliest relationships between them and continue throughout the marital union until they die. The young man should interrupt the woman's plans. He should pursue her with passion and purpose until she becomes a responder.

As a woman starts to initiate, she tends to pick up speed and moves easily into a vacuum of leadership. This slippery slope leads to deep mire. I am not saying that a woman should never initiate anything with a man or that a man should never respond to anything initiated by a woman. Rather, I am suggesting that a pattern of consistent initiation on the part of a woman and indifferent response on the part of a man may disrupt the divine plan for their life together.

A distinction is being made between biblical courtship (the practice of seeking a lady's favor and getting to know her by going through her father) and recreational dating (the independent decision of a man and woman to go out together). A father's involvement enables a young woman to put some distance between herself and a casual male acquaintance. Modesty and chastity call for warmth and friendliness without intimacy.[17] This biblical pattern establishes some clear protective boundaries emotionally, physically, and spiritually. If a couple do not honor God (which includes honoring parents) above all—including their own whims and desires, they are doomed to much tragedy and heartache.

Paige and I as childhood sweethearts did our first "dating" to the "kiddie show" with my sisters and brother as chaperones. We saw each other frequently at church and school activities, and Paige came to our home; but both of us knew that we were accountable to my father in the development of our friendship. Before Paige formally asked me to marry him, he asked my father for my hand in marriage. My sisters have been under the same guidance, and my brother followed this procedure when he sought a wife. Our son-in-love followed this same pattern.[18] A godly father will want his daughter to marry and leave when the right man comes for her in the right way.

WHAT CHILDREN WANT FROM THEIR PARENTS

Someone once quipped: Parents are out of a job by the time they are trained! Yet parents still try to prepare themselves to do the job. All qualities revealed in the lifestyle of children are eventually ascribed to their parents.[19] Genealogies set forth a family's line of honor. A son or daughter who is consistently disobedient will bring dishonor to an entire family.[20] Rebellion among teenagers was rare in the Old Testament—perhaps because after due process, the rebellious teen could be stoned to death.[21] There are no examples of this severe disciplinary action in Scripture, but this stern warning against rebellion must have been an effective deterrent to rebellious teens and a strong incentive to godly parents. I am not suggesting parents should resort to stoning or any other abusive behavior. However, young people need to be reminded that rebellion against parents, or any God-assigned authorities in their lives, is a serious offense. The sinful nature provides the potential for rebellion, but God can help anyone overcome that rebellion. Not only are rebellious children to be redeemed from spiritual separation from God, but they are also to be redeemed to family honor.

The stork was venerated in ancient cultures because it nourishes its parents. Nurtured by its parents, the stork never completely separates from mother and father but remains in contact with them into their old age. Feeling responsible to its parents, the bird seeks to repay that debt. Storks will nourish their offspring with exemplary affection and sit for such lengthy periods on their nests incubating their young that they lose their feathers. Storks will also bear on their backs the worn-out bodies of their parents, often offering them food from their own mouths. Storks feed their young and transport their parents.

LESSONS FOR CHILDREN

Jesus becomes an example for children. He chose to be subject to His parents. This subjection must have been difficult since His parents were not perfect. For whatever reasons God chose to put His Son in the home of imperfect parents. Children need to remember the example of Jesus when they decide that they have the wrong parents! God Himself chooses the parents to whom He delivers the precious gift of life. Just as Jesus willingly stepped under the umbrella of His parents' authority while He was growing up in their home, children today are expected to be in subjection to their parents—imperfect though they be.

As a child ages, the mandate to *obey* his parents becomes less important. Yet the command to *honor* them should remain. You honor parents by listening to what they are saying, by trying to understand their concerns, and by respecting their opinions. You ask questions for clarification; you look for motivation behind their directives. Your parents have been guardians protecting you and scouts looking out for what is best for you. Don't cast aside their years of rendering dedicated service for your moments of asserting personal rights.

Parents cannot wait for the childhood or teen years to prepare their children. Most experts affirm that the single biggest influence on a child is the quality of care he received in infancy and toddler days. During those early formative years, a child's character begins to be fashioned. The legacy of parents is a vital contributing factor in forming a personality and learning appropriate responses to the challenges of life. Although schools have begun to act as surrogate parents, for many generations children and young people received their education in the home from their own parents and/or tutors.

Godly parents do not seek power over their children to manipulate and control their lives. Discipline is not a means for parents to use in order to enforce arbitrary commands for their own benefit. Rather, discipline provides a loving way to train a child to obey the parent, who stands in the place of a loving Heavenly Father. Children will be trained—consciously or unconsciously—in some way. Godly parents seek to mold character, to inspire obedience, and to equip mind and heart for the challenges of life.

CHALLENGES TO OBEDIENCE

A child faces challenges in learning obedience—to his parents and then to God. First is his determination to go his own way. The book of Proverbs warns against this self-will repeatedly.[22]

Another testing for children and teens is the attraction and love they feel for the world. Wanting to dress without modesty like their peers, seeking to pursue entertainment without discernment, determining to twist and adapt virtues and principles to accommodate the modern age—these attachments to the secular world make godliness a difficult, if not impossible, goal.

Children have become conspicuously materialistic. Designer clothing and the latest electronic gadgets are at the top of their wish lists. Unfortunately, most are getting what they want because parents find it easier to shower them with gifts than to invest their time. When a family is enveloped in consumerism, even a child can lead by curbing spending, being satisfied with less, being more grateful, and distinguishing between needs and wants.

Pride also separates a child from his godly parents, from his spiritual roots, from an intimacy with God. Pride means there is no confession for sin, and without confession there is no changing of life and direction. Even agnosticism or atheism are possibilities when young people determine to leave God out of their lives, putting people or things or activities in first place in their hearts.

Godly parents will limit the exposure their children have to the values of the secular world. There are places their children will not go; there are movies they will not see; there is music to which they won't listen. Early they will learn the difference between right and wrong; they will be taught to be non-conformists in a culture that encourages conformity—a culture in which right is considered wrong and wrong is portrayed as right. Discerning children and teens know that sin has a price tag. Poor choices bring tragic consequences, and good character means holy influence. They will run to God when the world tries to draw them away.

Parents will also learn to stand in the shoes of their children—to see what they see and feel what they feel. This key to good parenting takes time, but it enables a parent to move forward with confidence and understanding in preparing a child for living in the world.

Children would do well to be aware that to isolate themselves from their parents and family not only means loneliness but also opens them to Satan's attack. They should be conscious of the protection of their parents' prayers and the strength of God's Word. They ought to be determined to step under the authority of their parents.

Postmodernism is one of the most effective weapons Satan has launched. The diverse selection of belief systems and religious choices has surpassed any previous generation. As if going through a cafeteria line, the individual caught in this system also picks and chooses whatever aspects of any religion seem right to him. Young people are especially vulnerable because they can please their parents by being active in the youth group of the local church, while choosing their own standard of morality according to what "feels" right for them.

Truth is no longer the objective rightness that stands outside your own experience; it becomes a creation from your personal perspective and a compilation from your own opinions on what is right for you. In essence, every opinion is right—if your experience has proven it right for you. Consequently, every opinion is to be respected. Each individual is self-sufficient and independent in finding his own way. Truth varies from person to person. The Bible is truth because you believe it. Morality is relative. What works for a young person may not work for his family, but both are right according to postmodern ideology. There is no absolute truth and certainly no guaranteed authority. Anyone seeking authority must earn it.

HOPE FOR A NEW GENERATION

Why would God expect children to hold their parents in honor and esteem? Shouldn't this reverence be reserved for God? *Honor* acknowledges a person's inestimable worth by means of words and actions. A child should recognize a debt of personal obligation to his parents. In translation from Hebrew or Greek, the word *honor* has the sense of "loving-kindness" or more simply "loyal love" and sometimes "mercy."[23] This virtue requires you to love and be loyal regardless of circumstances. Such obligations have little to do with what you personally want or don't want.

There is back-and-forth interaction among those in the family. Parents and children are unequal in their *positions* within the family. Parents initiated the obligation by giving life to the child, but what child can repay a parent for his life? Children are wise to speak well of their parents and to honor them by their own conduct.[24]

Children are born with a self-centered nature. I loved my babies devotedly, and they learned early to identify mother and to have special affection for me. However, they were not concerned for my health; they didn't care whether I had adequate rest; they didn't worry about whether I ate regular meals; they had no concern over whether I had time for relaxation and fun. As babies, they were concerned only with themselves—when they wanted attention, when they wanted to eat, when they felt like sleeping. If I had ignored that selfishness and allowed them to go their own way, they quickly would have learned to do just that.

The training process can be difficult and even unpleasant for parents as well as for children. It requires commitment and time. Parental obligations must often override personal comfort and fulfillment.

Television can be a corrupting influence because it exalts perversion, revels in infidelity, acknowledges divorce as a quick fix, accepts homosexuality, calls for anti-Americanism, takes lightly ridicule of God, and rejects religious faith and moral decency as unimportant. Television has also pulled members of the family away from fellowship and interaction with one another. Some homes have three TVs going, all tuned to the same station but located in different rooms so that each family member can watch the selected program alone. Too many families are living their lives in different rooms!

THE FUNCTION OF HOME

Parents and children would do well to remember the function of home as the magnetic force that holds the family together. The "wasting time at home" mentality is a destructive force on the family. If everyone is allowed to be busy doing his or her own thing, the family will slowly but surely be torn apart. Homes need to return to being a meaningful place of support and encouragement.

A family is built upon human relationships. Not only must parents develop relationships with their children, but children and teens should also make the effort to develop relationships with their parents. If often means a willingness to give up activities and even to bypass personal pursuits. Children and teens are painfully aware that no matter how much you love your family, there are times when you really don't like them! Biblical love is always a choice. It is not dependent upon personalities or circumstances. Genuine love is not a feeling; it is something you *do*. All the characteristics of love—compassion, kindness, humility, gentleness, and patience—are attitudes with which you choose to cover yourself.[25]

Another aspect of love is the commitment to work at keeping peace and resolving conflict or "bearing with one another in love."[26] Closely tied to forbearance is forgiveness. The world looks at the process of seeking forgiveness as a sign of weakness, but the Lord sees such humility as great strength. Relationships must also be more important than who did what when.[27] It remains true: The family that plays together, works together, and prays together will have the best chance to stay together. They will become a formidable support group for the challenges of the future.

REACHING OUT TO PARENTS

Teens can be willing participants in family gatherings planned by parents or other family members. They can also help create meaningful memories and plan happy celebrations for the family.

One of my happiest memories occurred when my parents celebrated their silver wedding anniversary. My sisters and brother joined me in preparing a surprise "This Is Your Life" celebration. We invited members of our extended family and friends—even from distant cities and other states. While our parents were out of the house, we set up a reception, including a wedding cake. Our parents sat in rocking chairs on their patio and listened to voices from the past. We took photographs, creating new memories while reliving happy experiences from the past. We said a public thank-you to our parents for the sacrificial investment they had made in our lives; we showcased the heritage and faith they had passed on to us; we had fun using our creativity and energies to plan a family event!

My husband was elected president of the Southern Baptist Convention in Salt Lake City, Utah. After it ended, our son Armour picked a scenic and quiet place for a brief outing. He asked our friend Heather to take a photograph of the three of us, which he later framed with this special verse: "The lines have fallen to me in pleasant places; yes, I have a good inheritance."[28] I am humbled and delighted with the sweet gratitude expressed.

Teens can also pick up the torch in spiritual pursuits. They can talk about the Lord within the family and in the interaction they have with their friends. They can make a conscious effort to be wise in the music they choose to play. They can make praise and worship part of their lifestyle—even outside the walls of the church. Even a teenager can start keeping a journal on the experiences of life, including recording prayer requests and answers. They can pray for members of the family.

Teens can do their part in preparing for and extending hospitality. They can invite their friends to enjoy the hospitality of their family, and they can assume responsibilities that help make that possible.

While our son Armour spent several years at Magnolia Hill doing some writing, he mingled with the students on our campus. He always seemed to find the ones who were lonely or who needed encouragement. When he saw someone who needed hospitality or when his dad announced that we needed to feed someone on campus, Armour was quick to volunteer to cook the meal. He is an excellent cook and prepares meals that are healthy and tasty. He would join our guests, willing to linger over coffee or tea. If we were out of town and someone appeared at the door, we knew Armour would feed and welcome him. Even his cooking does not compare with his welcoming hospitality.

Carmen learned that our church needed more homes to host Discipleship Now weekends for young people. She knew we had a heavy load of hospitality; she knew her daddy's very oppressive schedule; she knew that weekends were held in reserve for family as much as possible. But Carmen also knew that our home would be perfect for the weekend gathering. She did most of the work; she stayed up late and got up early to make it all come together. She has a warm heart for hospitality, and even from childhood she has been willing and eager to help me with cooking and cleaning to make our home a welcome center.

Children do reflect on their parents. Hannah prayed for a son, and God gave her Samuel. Hannah trained her son to obey; and when he joined Eli in the temple, he continued to be obedient. Therefore, God was able to use him as a mighty prophet. During the same time in Israel's history, the sons of Eli were disobedient and immoral. Undoubtedly Eli had taught his sons what was right, but he did not follow through with needed reproof and correction. Eli's sons ignored his teaching, and they died bringing shame on themselves and on Eli.[29] The home is a testing ground for spiritual disciplines. It is an ideal breeding ground for spiritual growth. Family members can be as effective as sandpaper to a rough edge.

WHAT MAKES A PERFECT PARENT?

Obviously an ideal parent from an adult perspective might take a different twist than the ideal from a kid's point of view. After all, "generation gap" is a logical and accurate description of the bridge that stretches between parent and child.

Would anyone disagree that love is the deepest need for teens. Don't we all need someone who cares; someone who loves unconditionally. Listening is another longing from a world obsessed with busyness. Teens need a prolonged listening ear. Integrity is sadly missing, and kids recognize veneer; they want transparency in their parents—what you see is what you get.

Kids also like parents who can lighten up. They are already uptight and stressed out with peer pressures and adult expectations. They need to see a sense of humor. They need parents who don't take themselves or anyone else too seriously.

Kids need parents, not just pals. That means leadership. Limits need to be clearly set, but kids need to extend decision making. They need to have respect. More and more they need reasoned responses and the opportunity to present their points of view. But they still long for someone to be in charge and responsible!

Home is designed by God as the place where a child can find unconditional love, tender care, and unquestioned forgiveness. Home is a shelter from the cares of the world, a reservoir of happy memories, and peace in the midst of chaos.

1. Gen. 1:26–28; Ps. 127:3–5; 128:3–6.
2. Gen. 48:16; 2 Sam. 18:18.
3. Deut. 28:4.
4. Gen. 30:1–24; 1 Sam. 1.
5. Matt. 18:1–5; Mark 10:13–16.
6. Eph. 6:1–4.
7. Exod. 20:12; Deut. 5:16.
8. Eph. 6:1–3.
9. Lev. 19:3; Deut. 16:18–18:22.
10. 1 Sam. 8:1–5.
11. Luke 15:11–24.
12. See Tom Allen, booklet "Hope for Hurting Parents" (Camp Hill, PA: Christian Publications, 1999).
13. From Hebrew *banah,* meaning "to build."
14. 1 Cor. 8:13.
15. 1 Cor. 10:23.
16. 1 Cor. 10:31.
17. Douglas Wilson, *Her Hand in Marriage* (Moscow, ID: Canon Press, 1997).

18. See the story of Carmen and Mark in my book *BeAttitudes for Women* (Nashville: Broadman & Holman Publishers, 2000).

19. Deut. 23:2; Isa. 57:3; Ezek. 16:44; Matt. 11:16–17.

20. See the behavior of Absalom with regard to his father David in 2 Sam. 13–18.

21. Deut. 21:18–21.

22. Prov. 22:6.

23. Hebrew *hesed* and Greek *eleios*.

24. Bruce Malina, *Windows on the World of Jesus* (Louisville: Westminster/John Knox Press, 1993), 108–109.

25. Col. 3:12–14; 1 Cor. 13:1–13.

26. Eph. 4:2–3.

27. Matt. 6:15.

28. Ps. 16:6.

29. 1 Sam. 2:12, 23–24, 29; 3:13–14.

7

The Grandparents' Heritage

BONDS BETWEEN GRANDPARENTS and grandchildren require an investment of time and energy. Care for both the young and the elderly should spring from within the family. Among the Jews, the family, more than the synagogue, has been the primary bridge for the transmission of Judaism from generation to generation.

The treasures grandparents bring to a family can be easily neglected or even lost and forgotten. The loving investment of grandparents in the lives of their grandchildren can never be an adequate substitute for parental responsibility. Nor should adult children rob their own parents of well-deserved rest and retirement in their later years. On the other hand, as parents seek to rear their children, their parents should have wise counsel to help them fulfill the responsibilities of parenthood. They can also expect their parents to experience joy and delight in being involved with their grandchildren on a regular basis. With reasonable and consistent effort, a family will often find examples of bedrock faith and virtuous character in its ancestry to pass to the coming generations.

There is no better way to teach moral truths than to tell stories about people whose lives actually matched up with what they said. They consistently "walked their talk." Especially is that meaningful when they are people from whom you descended through the generations.

My father, Charles Kelley, was elected president of his high school class. He never campaigned for the office. He didn't even have the money to attend class parties because he grew up in a large and humble family during the depression. After school and on Saturdays he worked at the local hardware store to contribute to the family income. He wasn't a likely candidate for winning a popular election. However, he was honest and hardworking and considerate of others. His classmates admired and respected him. After a year of service, they decided that Charles Kelley did such a good job as president he ought to be re-elected, and so he was year by year throughout high school. I didn't know of this phenomenon until my dad and I visited during his recuperation from cancer surgery. But I was already aware of the confidence he inspired in people, of his sensitivity to others, of his commitment to responsibilities, and of his awesome work ethic. All these together enabled him to build a widely respected family business and watch it prosper for half a century.

HANDED-DOWN WISDOM

To forget your ancestors breaks the connecting cord with the past and the lessons to be learned therefrom. Often such negligence pushes you into a sea of self-indulgence and self-centeredness that allows individual selfishness free rein. On the other hand, to learn from those who have gone before can fortify you against your own foolish or destructive impulses.

Family members have many ways to stay in touch and keep their heritage alive. In chain letters one person writes a note and sends it; the next person reads it and adds her own news and greetings and sends it to still another. If you commute to work or drive long distances, communicate with family members or record family history via a tape recorder. Keep your relationship with your grandchildren alive by sending them videotapes of your everyday activities. We did a video of my husband with his dogs. Bandit (a Treeing Walker Hound), alias "the Squealer," is "singing" to an accompaniment of the harmonica; then he is sitting behind the Big Daddy's presidential desk; he even climbs a tree on the campus. Noche (the black Labrador Retriever) joins the "Squealer" for a romp with the Big Daddy. Abigail and Rebekah will love seeing their beloved grandfather with these two crazy canines!

Putting your voice on tape or your likeness on video, reading a story, or just sharing an armchair visit with a family member far away are wonderful investments of time and energy. Tapes should not be a substitute for regular telephone calls, during which you can respond to questions and enjoy voice contact in a more intimate way. Nor should you abandon every effort to make trips to see your children and grandchildren.

Grandparents must often take the initiative to visit or be available for baby-sitting. I make frequent trips to Louisville to see Abi and Beka. The Big Daddy and I host our granddaughters here at Magnolia Hill while their parents get away. I completely clear my calendar, and my husband rearranges his schedule so that we can immerse ourselves in the lives of our granddaughters during those precious days! We want to make happy reunions a regular part of our relationship to our granddaughters.

To see virtues and values in the character of actual people, and especially when those people are your ancestors, makes a strong claim upon your life. It could even be a tool for restoring morality to what is rapidly becoming an amoral society. Analyzing the patterns of your past may help you deal more effectively with the present so that you move to the future with greater wisdom and discernment. To take time to examine your life periodically enables you to recall God's faithfulness, to learn from your mistakes, and to find the courage to move forward. More often than not, the key players who helped you direct your faith journey are members of your own family. Families provide a natural support system of loving, caring, giving, and sharing.

In our family, I create *ebenezers* (the Hebrew transliteration of two words meaning "stone of help"). I want our children and grandchildren to remember the blessings God has given to our family. I want them to relive happy experiences. For our children I created countless albums and scrapbooks.

When Carmen graduated from high school, I gathered scattered photos and brought her albums up to date. The project got my juices flowing so that I put together a surprise "This Is Your Life" open house, reliving special memories of her childhood and teen years! Memory points were set up throughout the house with scrapbooks and photo albums as well as mementos collected through the years, such as the video of her baptism by her father in Israel's Jordan River. Her friends enjoyed the trip down memory lane, and most of them shared some special story about Carmen on video for her future enjoyment.

Now I am working on the grandchildren. I can do a better job for them. I can afford to purchase specialty albums and accessories to enhance my creativity as well as take and process lots of photographs. Abigail's album is up to date, including inscriptions; and Rebekah's album has been started. I will enjoy these albums and share them with the girls during their visits to Magnolia Hill. I plan to give the albums to them when they graduate from high school. I have also started a journal for each of the girls to record my own observations of their childhood.

Kathryn Monday, mother of seven and grandmother of seventeen, is a writer, painter, and serious gardener in Spirit Lake, Idaho. She describes "the Book," a volume she has prepared for her own family to record their heritage. In her table of contents is a chapter for each generation, including birth and death certificates, marriage records, any available biographical information, photographs from birth to death, family record sheets, copies of any pertinent documents (military service, spiritual events like baptism, final will and testament, property deeds). She has a section of maps with highlighted areas of interest at the end of each chapter. Monday's volume begins with the oldest person and ends with her own grandchildren. She concludes with a section on family achievements.

Monday found notable people in her family, both past and present—authors, artists, inventors, entertainers, athletes. To document these achievements, she included news articles, book jackets, photographs, poems, and even a few short manuscripts. The carefully prepared index for these three hundred pages required a big investment of time, but its contents make the volume user-friendly.

Monday duplicated a high-quality copy of its pages for her entire family. The printer drilled holes for fastening clips, enabling the family to add to the book in the future. Monday plans to send each family member an update sheet for recording births, deaths, and interesting things that happened during the preceding year so she can enter these items on family record sheets and make helpful additions as long as she is able.

How easy it is to miss many wonderful memories when a project is put off for some future date, allowing generations to pass without a record of their lives and work. Bringing the past alive with real people is wonderful in any setting, but it takes on a special delight and purpose when that setting is the family. Genealogy is a fascinating study that strengthens the family.[1]

My mother has written her life's story with vignettes and anecdotes from our family through the years. It is an awesome task to put on paper almost eight decades, but she has faithfully worked at preparing for her children and grandchildren a testimony of her life and faith. She included photographs and special documents. During a Christmas reunion, Mother presented a copy of this precious volume to each child and grandchild. What a treasure!

There are many mediums through which you can record genealogy and family events. When my husband completed his second year of service as president of the Southern Baptist Convention, we hosted the annual dinner for past presidents of the Convention and selected a gift for each. With the help of our wonderful Magnolia Hill support staff and the creativity of some special Baptist ladies, a unique, handmade quilt was prepared for each former president. The quilts were imprinted with photographs, a record of Convention service, and a favorite verse of Scripture.

The quilts were hung in the room where our dinner was served so that all could enjoy the memories of each. Everyone seemed delighted! But my pleasure had just begun! When I returned to our suite, I found another quilt and cushion from my sweet colaborer Bobbi Moosbrugger, who with her mother and sister-in-law had fashioned the other quilts. This quilt was imprinted with precious photographs of our extended family—a unique "family tree"—and the cushion had likenesses of all our family dogs, who, as any who know us would be aware, are very much a part of the family! What precious and unique treasures to add to our home as ornaments of beauty and aesthetically pleasing historical archives for our family!

TRADITIONS OR TRENDS

The link between generations is largely forged through family traditions that reaffirm the bonds between husbands and wives, between parents and children, between the dead and the living. Traditions, especially those your children can see, hear, feel, smell, and taste, will provide vivid memories on which parents can build from year to year. If there is not a conscious effort to build timeless traditions, the family may be pulled away by whatever trends are in vogue at the moment. Then a void may develop in which bedrock faith and solid family values are replaced with contemporary fads. The roots of a family foundation are exchanged for the rootlessness of peer pleasures. Convenience overwhelms commitment, and family responsibility falls to personal rationalization.

My husband and I took our children to annual meetings of the Southern Baptist Convention. We would have been less encumbered without them, but to involve them in this annual event that was so much a part of our lives and ministry provided another natural link between them and us. They had opportunity to meet our partners in ministry, listen to the boring business sessions enough to see the unfolding history, and even occasionally enjoy some humor. We had meals together; we shared hotel rooms; and either before or after the Convention, we managed to work in a family outing in the Convention city. They developed friendships among those attending and looked forward to renewing those friendships annually. It was a tradition that espoused both what was boring and uninteresting with what was fun and exciting. Isn't that a microcosm of life itself?

Parents often err in believing that they should include their children only when the children can be entertained. Children will learn early that life is a mixture of drudgery and excitement, of privilege and responsibility, of waiting and going, of choosing what I want to do and willingly participating in what someone else wants to do.

RITUALS

Rituals within the family not only provide a tool for bonding among family members, but they also serve as a developmental tool for rearing the next generation. They add structure and security for children as they develop physically, mentally, emotionally, and spiritually. They bring comfort because every member of the family remembers those mundane acts around which everything else revolves. Families tend to ritualize what is important to them. Although family sayings may be known to outsiders, the origin and primary message are often hidden from all but the family.

Rituals set the family apart in unique fellowship since some family traditions are too special for public display. Weekends have always been a haven for our family rituals. When our children were young, Saturday mornings were sacred—no alarm clocks, no meetings, no guests (until Mr. Wilson came along!). We all looked forward to sleeping until we awakened naturally. Then the children played with their father while I prepared brunch. We did vary our menu some, but it was always a full, hot breakfast. Pancakes or waffles or French toast were the favorites and were served most frequently. There were at least two courses and a "side" dish. China and glassware, tablecloth or placemats, and garnished plates were the order of the day.

One Saturday morning about nine o'clock, as we were rolling out of bed, the doorbell rang. A retired widower from our church, whom we met that morning for the first time, stood at the door with his arms full of groceries. We were buying our first home and carrying a double mortgage because of the necessary down payment. Since the grocery allotment in our austere budget was the first place to cut when unexpected expenses appeared, we welcomed the revival of the unselfish and generous custom of "pounding" the preacher by providing staples for his cupboard.

We learned that Mr. Wilson, who was retired from the food business, had selected three or four members of the church staff to receive his weekly bounty (ice cream, pastrami and a variety of other meats, special fruits—always things we would not buy for ourselves except for the gallon of milk). He didn't stay long that first morning, and in the succeeding weeks he always came at a later hour. Soon he pulled up a chair and joined us for brunch. We let him know if we were going out of town, and he called us if he became ill or if the weather prohibited his travel. Until he died, Mr. Wilson was our special and exclusive Saturday morning guest. Paige and I looked forward to his visit as much as the children did, not just for the groceries but to enjoy his stories and feel his love!

After Mr. Wilson died, we moved to a new neighborhood. The children were in college. The routine changed, but the ritual continued. When everyone was awake and dressed, we went to a restaurant specializing in breakfast and brunch. At a leisurely pace, we ordered from the menu, ate our favorite foods, and lingered over coffee and tea with happy conversation and memory flashbacks.

Then we moved to Magnolia Hill in North Carolina. As the children come and go, we continue the ritual of Saturday brunch while adapting it to the times. When our son Armour was in residence, on Saturday morning he and I prepared a gourmet feast with an egg dish, cooked grain, meat, and hot, made-from-scratch popovers or biscuits, accompanied by freshly squeezed orange juice and freshly ground coffee. We spent several hours at the table, savoring every morsel and talking endlessly about the events of the week—all on the side porch if weather permitted.

Rituals are a way to bring meaningful tasks back into the home. They help to define the heart of family commitment and intimacy, setting apart the home as an important place for dealing with all the issues of life.

When Armour was nine years of age, I accompanied him on a mission trip to England. We stayed with the Sapworths in a suburb of London. Armour had daily assignments in public school classrooms. In the evening we attended preaching services. In the late afternoon our hostess served buttered bread and a strong brew of loose-leaf tea. We talked about the events of the day and received refreshment to prepare us for the evening assignment. Such was our introduction to the British afternoon tea ritual. After Armour and I returned to Dallas, we continued having tea in the afternoon, a leisurely time for us to enjoy each other's company until his athletic schedule made it impossible to do so.

Through the years I have become addicted to that afternoon renewal experience. I have had tea in hotels and tea rooms throughout the world, but the dearest time is still here at Magnolia Hill in our garden room with freshly brewed loose-leaf tea, tomato and buffalo cheese sandwiches, homemade scones, imported Devon cream, and perhaps a shortbread cookie. With chamber music playing softly and family members gathered around, nothing is any more precious!

Home must be not only a place for meaningless relaxation during a retreat from the real world; rather the home should be the center of the world—a place for productivity as well as retreat. Family members need to be continually drawn home to refresh and recommit themselves to the deeper meaning of life.

Rituals can be tied to the seasons. The winter lends itself to evenings with a roaring fire and a hot beverage before bedtime; spring may introduce having the evening meal on the side porch; summer may mean traveling with Daddy on the weekends and no alarm clocks in the mornings; fall may mean using the Thanksgiving and Christmas china for family meals. These are seasonal rituals for our family. Waiting for the appropriate season seems to heighten the pleasure and make the experience even more special when the moment of passage occurs.

FAMILY GATHERINGS AND CELEBRATIONS

Family reunions are wonderful settings in which both sweet and bitter memories are awakened. You are reminded of who you are and from whence you came as well as where you are going! They inspire you to remember, reminisce, recall, and even relive the past, which can become a wonderful springboard for the future. Even bitter memories have a way of putting everything into perspective. Whether a wedding, birthday, anniversary, or even a funeral—a reunion of family members can restore a sense of identity or reconnect ties that may have been broken.

Holidays, too, are perfect opportunities for family members to reach out and touch one another. No one enjoys celebrations as thoroughly as families who love one another and enjoy one another's company. Those celebrations do not have to be confined to holidays but should extend to personal special events—birthdays, anniversaries, awards, and recognitions.

For two decades our extended family has enjoyed "theme" Christmas celebrations. I guess this idea originated with me. Planning our Christmas family gathering has always been a big event. It was fun to get the creative juices flowing and mark the seasonal gathering with some special memories. Our international travel was my nudge to venture into this Christmas theme planning. It was relatively easy to pick up props—decorations and gifts—and plan menus and activities in connection with the time spent in interesting countries of the world.

During a month "down under" at the turn of the millennium, I gathered props for decorations, gifts, menus, and games from Australia and New Zealand. Other themes seemed to evolve from ethnic celebrations. For example, travel in England also produced our Beatrix Potter Christmas. Those decorations once enjoyed in the Christmas season have now been recycled to the Easter season.

Easter, too, lends itself to celebration for the Christian community, just as Passover awakens family celebration in Jewish homes. I have a wonderful set of Easter eggs that provide for my family a show-and-tell on the events of the resurrection. I have filled each egg with a Scripture verse and some item that is inspired by the verse.

Our Passover Box is also a reminder of the deliverance of the children of Israel from their bondage in Egypt.[2] The kit helps kids and adults relive the story of Passover with a real script and props like Pharaoh's hat, Miriam's headpiece, Moses' beard, plus toy frogs, bugs, wild animals, locusts, and hail. These objects enable parents to share with their children the events demonstrating the providence of the Lord. Family fun is great, but more important is a reminder of a family's spiritual heritage.

You can add small embellishments to the ordinary details of your family life by looking for everyday happenings you can turn into serendipity occasions. When my children were in the university, I regularly sent them care packages, especially during exam periods or on Valentine's Day or prepackaged birthday kits with cake, colorful napkins and plates, party favors for their friends, packages to be opened.

For my son's college graduation and then again on his thirtieth birthday, I printed and circulated an edition of the *Armour Star Times*—a newspaper with stories and poems he had written, vignettes from his life, a timeline of major events, articles about him by his peers and family, pictures from athletic contests and hunting expeditions. This paper is another *ebenezer*, a "stone of help" to store memories from three decades of his life.

Mark and Carmen's wedding is celebrated again and again. Not only did we make a video to preserve that happy event, but we also encased the top of the wedding cake in a keepsake dome. We have a wonderful photograph album, and Carmen's dress has been carefully preserved for the future. When my sister Eileen married, we took the silk flower bouquet Carmen carried as a bridesmaid and put it in a shadow box with a photograph of the wedding party to remind Carmen of that special event.

Celebrations can cost money, and they demand an investment of time. To be really special, they must also be marked by creativity in using what you have and by sensitivity to what is important to your family members. But they are indeed worth the effort as one of the most effective ways to say "I love you" and "I think you are important." In the midst of daily pressures, economic challenges, and vanishing time, celebrations can be an opportunity for refreshing renewal for the family.

CONCLUSION

Family members are those among whom you can be yourself. You don't have to try to impress family. There is no fee to belong; you have a lifetime membership. There is no test to pass; you are woven into the warp and woof of the fabric itself. You have a right to be included just because of who you are. However, within the family there is little room for superficiality or phoniness; nor can you get away with an arrogant, "better than you" attitude. They knew you back when; they know you best now; and they are unimpressed with any airs you may assume.

Offering unconditional love is still the most precious gift you can give to children, grandchildren, and to every family member. Parents and grandparents are uniquely situated to provide a role model for a good and godly lifestyle. They do this by transmitting a knowledge of those who have gone before but even more by their personal example of how they are living day by day. I want to devote my energies and creativity to showing the world how the one-of-a-kind design in Abigail and Rebekah will change what on the surface may seem to be ordinary granddaughters into extraordinary young women who will strive for and reach their greatest potential.

I intend to be a better grandparent than I was a parent! I have had more experience; I am more aware of my own strengths and weaknesses; I know more about what children need to make it in the world. I can share duties with their parents. I'm going to have more fun! I spend far more *unstructured* time with my grandchildren than I did with my children. I don't have to concentrate on the mundane basics; I can devote my energies and creativity to enriching their lives!

1. Kathryn Monday, "Finding My Story," *The Family in America,* vol. 8 (Mount Morris, IL: Rockford Institute, August 1993), 6–8.

2. Produced by *Aish HaTorah,* 11418 Old Georgetown Road, North Bethesda, MD 20852.

8

Biblical Principles for Rearing Children

AMAZINGLY, EVEN WITH THE FAMILY under continual attack, the percentage of teenagers believing that a good marriage and family life is "very important" has increased.[1] The most loving thing a mother and father can do for a child is to let him see that they love one another. Being a good husband or wife, just as being a good parent, takes time and effort. If you are too busy to invest energies and creativity in couple time as well as in family time, you are busier than God wants you to be. Priorities need to be rearranged!

LIVING A PATTERN FOR MARRIAGE

Parents must provide good models of what Christian marriage ought to be. Husbands and wives must be committed to a growing, healthy relationship with one another. They ought to exhibit a strong, loving relationship in which they complement one another and show the noblest and best expression of love. This breeds security and helps their children to develop and mature. As their children's most effective teachers, they have the best chance to pass on a pattern for biblical marriage.

A number of troubling social trends are the result of the decline and sabotage of marriages. Children reared without a married mother and father are more likely to be poor, to use drugs, to drop out of school or to fail academically, to be abused, or to develop chronic health problems. Children from homes broken by divorce are more likely to go through divorce themselves, to become unwed parents, or to be incarcerated for crimes.[2]

Most experts agree that this generation is experiencing a staggering decrease in parental or adult supervision of children. A parent committed to investing time and energy in the development of a child often must accept a lower standard of living, standing against a materialistic society that praises workaholism and the acquisition of things far more than it honors the rearing of children. Ruth Spencer is a talented hairstylist in Wake Forest, North Carolina. As a single parent, she limits her hours of work in order to have more time with her son. That means less income and intense hours when she is working. But she is committed to place her parenting responsibilities above her professional pursuits. I appreciate that!

Theodore Roosevelt was solidly committed to his wife and family. A book written about him and the priorities in his life is entitled *A Bully Father.* Letters from his children reveal that Christmas mornings he and his wife Edith invited their six children into their bedroom to empty their stockings and open their presents—even when they lived in the White House. No one questioned that he put his family first, no matter what!

A careful look at the absence of character in the workplace, as well as a careful consideration of the low productivity that inevitably accompanies a poor work ethic, is a nudge to take another look at the values of the coming generation. Today's children, as tomorrow's workers, should be the most important national product on the scene. The responsibility of family life not only is honored as a valuable biblical principle, but it also becomes the mark of good business.

Statisticians are reporting the marriage rate at an unprecedented low and the divorce rate at an all-time high. Mothers are increasingly moving their primary energies out of the home and into the labor force, and America is facing a generation of children who have spent more time in institutional care than under parental supervision.

Secular experts in psychology, sociology, and other disciplines, as well as religious leaders, have noted that the family is the central and most important unit of society. Its potency to maintain order in the community and shape the next generation is more an empirical fact than a private observation. This potential influence extends beyond the border of the family to affect those who rub shoulders with its members. No other force is so effective in shaping the physical, emotional, mental, and moral aspects of behavior for a human being than the family that gives birth, nurtures, and molds the character of those passing through its gates.

Families then have a choice of either awakening the best and restraining the worst or unleashing the worst and sabotaging the best in those who are a part of the family. There is no better setting for building camaraderie, achieving cooperation, inspiring selflessness and sacrifice, and finding unity of purpose.

Marriage, as discussed more extensively in chapter 2, is central to the family. The uniting of one man and one woman in a lifelong, exclusive, monogamous relationship is the beginning of a family. Within this union love can be expressed in its noblest and highest model. This marital love is important for children as well as for husbands and wives.

Fathers and mothers are challenged to work together to form the most effective teaching unit for their children. They must prepare their children to take their own places in the world, forming the families of the next generation. Whatever the family now is, society will become. Parents must faithfully *show* their children what they ought to do and how they ought to live rather than trying to *tell* them or *make* them do certain things.

A consensus of wisdom is clear: It is more important for your child to see consistent expression of your love for your spouse than to see expressions of your love for him. That is not to say that expressing love to your child is unimportant; it is simply to remind parents that a child needs to see that his father and mother love each other. A wife whose husband has become busy with his professional pursuits becomes lonely, and she may be neglected. The message of indifference she receives is also transmitted to the child.

One of the most important lessons to be taught by parents is the responsibility and reward of an exclusive sexual relationship. Too often contemporary sexual views suggest that any sexual encounter is merely a personal decision and that monogamy is just a lifestyle choice in which consequences and risks are to be borne by the individual alone. The rampant epidemic of AIDS and other sexually transmitted diseases with documented fallout spilling over to innocent victims within the family has certainly proven the fallacy of that position. The risk to immediate and extended family and society at large is clear. The innocent often pay with their own lives for the choices of others.

Promiscuity has preoccupied today's society and instigated moral anarchy. When sexuality is considered pleasure alone, children soon become an inconvenience or obstacle to pleasure. Not only does the birth rate drop, as it has in the last two decades, but also abortion and sterilization become by-products and tools to propagate libertinism. In addition to turning away from bearing and rearing children, couples experience a lessening of parental instinct. They are willing to settle for custodial care of their children while pursuing careers and social pleasures.

Putting before your children a pattern for monogamy within marriage is important:

- Although morality ultimately cannot be regulated, a government dedicated to the good of its people can prohibit what is destructive to the family—polygamy, sodomy, and prostitution.
- Provision of a strong economy and protection of the weakest members of society comes through joint holding of property in marriage and by tax exemptions available for dependents.
- Establishment of continuity with preceding and succeeding generations comes by building an exclusive unit.

The pattern for Christian marriage and the framework of a godly family life fashion the cocoon in which you are going to rear your children. They need to be a part of all you do. They should participate in your ups and downs so that they can see how you respond and react to adversities, challenges, and difficulties as well as to successes.

TEACHING SPIRITUAL TRUTHS

The parent is his child's teacher in the sense of nurturing the child's academic capabilities and facilitating his learning experience. Instead of encouraging meaningless activities with their children's peers, such as unsupervised and unlimited television viewing or unrestricted computer access, parents must be committed to provide their offspring with time together as a family. First and foremost must be the teaching of values, which ought to be fashioned by parents after a careful study of Scripture. Parents develop the character of their children by teaching them guidelines for living a godly life and boundaries for healthy relationships.

Teaching involves giving instruction and showing a child how to do a task. Children learn everything best through observing and imitating. A child will be shaped from his birth by the way his parents live before him. Sometimes the child's proficiency is imparted by teaching or drilling. The parent may choose to involve others—from the public or private sector—in the educational process, or he may elect to deliver the education himself through the venue of homeschooling.

The apostle Paul commended the mother and grandmother of Timothy, his own protégé, because of the importance they assigned to Timothy's childhood education. Paul recognized that whatever investment he had made in Timothy, the young man's spiritual moorings were built on the foundation of truth he learned in his childhood home.[3] Timothy had a godly mother and grandmother who passed to him that heritage of faith. In a real sense Timothy's godly home prepared him to live in an ungodly world! Parents must diligently build boundaries of loving protection around their children—the most priceless treasure God gives.

Parents must begin a child's spiritual formation by teaching him the Bible. Its stories, its truths, its applications—all must be incorporated into the learning experience. As the revelation of an all-knowing God, the Bible provides absolute truth. That includes all you need to know about the parenting task and rearing and nurturing your children in the Lord—information about children, family life, values, training, discipline. Neither taking your child to a synagogue or church nor placing him in a religious school for his general education is enough. The knowledge transmitted must permeate the child's entire life, and he must have the opportunity under the careful supervision of his parents to apply the facts he has learned in everyday life experiences.

Parents have a multifaceted task. They are to shepherd their children to an understanding of themselves and how they fit into God's world, and they are to teach their children obedience to authorities in their lives. Children are not to be robots controlled in thought and action by someone else or automatons obsessed with their own autonomy. Parents must not mold their children to a personal agenda or allow them to take the slippery slope of convenience that leads to being squeezed into the mold of the world. Rather they are to act as agents of the Lord in guiding their children along the pathway God has placed before them. The parent is a guide in helping the child to understand himself and the world in which he lives.

Once a child learns the truth in Scripture, he is ready to move toward commitment to those truths.[4] Wisdom in itself is not enough. Solomon received the greatest gift of wisdom ever bestowed on a mortal man. This wisdom is evident in his writings in the Old Testament. However, he completely messed up his life and assured the end of the United Kingdom of Israel. He received wisdom, but he was not faithful to use *discernment* in appropriating that wisdom.

Moses, in preparing a new generation to enter the Promised Land, emphasized the importance of the home in teaching truth and obedience. He assigned two primary responsibilities to God-fearing parents.

First, parents were instructed to hear God's Word themselves and then to apply that Word to their own lives: "Hear, O Israel, The LORD our God is one Lord. Love the Lord your God with all your heart and with all your soul and with all your strength. These commandments that I give you today are to be upon your hearts."[5] The truth of God was to be so established in the parent's heart that it would draw him into a proper relationship with God. Without that personal relationship with God, a parent could not communicate the truths of God to his children. To pass on something worthwhile to your children, you must first possess it yourself.

Second, parents are to incorporate these spiritual truths in their family circle. If the truths are central in the hearts of the parents, they will fill the home as well. Moses offered two ways of communicating these truths to children: specific teaching and general talking. There is no teaching without planned, formal instruction—a time and a place and a curriculum! No one can teach without first being taught. Parents themselves must determine to study and learn God's Word. Only when they have learned can they pass its truths to their children. Specific teaching is usually done in family worship—set-apart times for the family to come together and hear God's Word read and explained.

Specific teaching is not enough. Parents must maximize every means of communication, even simple talking and ordinary conversation. Spontaneous instruction should occur as part of everyday living. Many experiences in family life lend themselves to teaching spiritual truths. Some of the most valuable lessons come in the natural course of events and provide a way to flesh out biblical principles. Moses describes this lifestyle teaching clearly—as you walk, stand, sit, or lie down!

Modern society seems to be pushing God out of classrooms. When a void is created, something else inevitably moves in. Outside influences have a part in what is happening to your children. But how do children get to movie theaters to view R-rated flicks? How do they receive and view pornography on the Internet undetected? How do they fill their time listening to ungodly music and watching questionable television shows? Parents must be proactive not only in protecting their children from degrading influences but also in making available what is good and wholesome for their children.

Music is a powerful medium that has the potential for emotional, moral, physical, and spiritual influence over the family. However, music cannot be selected solely according to personal taste and preference; rather, it needs to pass under the magnifying glass of Scripture and through the sieve of godly discernment. Recently a CD recorded by the Knight Family Singers (parents and six children ages two to twenty-one years) came to my desk. Entitled "Harmony at Home," the CD bears testimony to the importance of home in this family. The Knights have learned that no matter where their physical residence may be, they can dwell at home "in their hearts" with the Lord.

These parents adopted biblical principles as their "construction and maintenance tools" for building their dwelling place. They have used music as a bond for drawing their family into fellowship and as a means of worshiping God. They provide their own accompaniment with classical guitar, celtic harp, and piano; some of the songs are their own compositions. How blessed I am to hear the harmonious and melodious music wafting through our home. How encouraged I am to know that Paige and I taught biblical principles and lived an example for marriage and family life before Lennie B. and Richard Knight during their days in the university.

Moral relativism is at the heart of postmodernism. It brings a steady diet of sexual promiscuity and perversion, media violence, personal autonomy, and the denial of biblical principles. When parents remove themselves from their children's lives and become spiritually sterile, blatantly materialistic, and overwhelmingly self-centered, what will awaken their sensitivities to the dangers facing their own offspring? Should we be surprised when children and young people are unable to distinguish reality from fantasy or right from wrong?

Parents do indeed have a responsibility to rear their own children. Parenting is not buying your children anything they want and hiring babysitters, nannies, guardians or imposing on grandparents to supervise their activities. Parenting is not putting your children in the best private school with all the extracurricular activities you can squeeze in. Rather, parenting means spending time with your children and teens in order to teach them truth, to help them learn the difference between right and wrong, and to nurture them into a happy and productive adult life.

Children don't need more day care, more after-school care, more counseling, more entertainment. They need more parental love and guidance. Parents must make the family their first priority. Parents can counteract bad influences by becoming proactive—investing time in their own children!

Only through specific teaching (planned times for instruction) and spontaneous talking (unexpected moments for reinforcing virtues and values) can parents unleash the power of the Word of God so that it influences a child's thoughts and actions throughout life, including private moments as well as public actions.

Deuteronomy also describes the way parents were to place God's Word in their homes.[6] Phylacteries were to be worn on the hand and arm as a symbol of reaching to the heart, and frontlets were to be placed between the eyes as a symbol of controlling thought life. Mention is made of the *mezuzah,* the small piece hung on doorposts to remind the family that God's Word should govern even the most intimate areas of family life. Both the phylacteries (small leather boxes) and the *mezuzah* (small, decorative cylinder of metal, pottery, or porcelain) contained a portion of Scripture to remind everyone of the pervasive influence of God's Word.

Maintaining a time of family worship is one of the most effective ways to promote the importance of spiritual formation. This formal expression of religious training and nurture within the home takes determination and creativity on the part of parents. It does not negate the importance of lifestyle teaching. It is a precious privilege to introduce your children to the Heavenly Father and a wonderful fail-safe measure to set apart your offspring unto the Lord. It becomes a time to acquaint all in the family circle with God and to enjoy sweet communion with Him.

Daily worship within the family is important, and it is service to God—a means of glorifying Him and extending the virtues of His kingdom to a pagan world. A time must be selected and protected so that nothing interferes with its practice. Prayers must be offered up, and time must be set aside to wait for a Word from the Lord in quietness and openness. Praise and thanksgiving ought to be given, and His Word should be read and discussed. A private fire for God within family worship can break into a growing flame of service for God.

One of the greatest barriers to family worship is overcommitment. It takes time to build relationships with one another, and it takes time for a family to build a relationship with God. If a time of family gathering is geared to the convenience of when it feels right and when it fits into everyone's schedule, the occasion will lose its value. Genuine commitment must surpass feeling and circumstances. The events of any given day, important at the time, may not even be remembered the next day or the following week or in a year's time. Nevertheless, spiritual nurture will take root and be a part of the very foundation of life.

Children are God's assignment to parents. When your child leaves home, he should have a worldview that is God centered rather than man-centered. A parent is not finished when a child's actions have been brought into line with family expectations. Rather, parents are entrusted with the task of giving beyond familial goals to do spiritual formation—developing a child's belief system according to God's Word. If you have concentrated only on your child's actions, he will conform to your expectations as long as he is under your care and control; but when your control is over, he then will follow his own convictions.

The child should be sharp and well-fashioned because he is destined to be an arrow of the Lord on the spiritual battlefield. He is commissioned to pass on a godly heritage to the next generation just as you have entrusted it to him. Family worship must go beyond the perfunctory expression of thanks to God for food at mealtime. Each family member should have a copy of the Bible as well as other devotional and inspirational literature.

During family worship time, you should talk of God in a natural way and discuss what the Bible teaches about personal character and daily living. Children should learn firsthand that prayer is a means of communicating with God, even about the most mundane aspects of life.

My husband and I also use our home as a gathering place for friends from around the world so that our children, and now our grandchildren, can experience fellowship and friendship with people from a variety of ethnic backgrounds and cultures. We like to serve ethnic foods and talk about the different cultures and customs of people from all over the world. This international hospitality is coupled with a determination to make it possible for our children to visit other countries and immerse themselves in cultures unlike their own.

Our son Armour, while in high school, spent six weeks in Uganda teaching basketball clinics; he lived several months in Israel visiting archaeological and biblical sites; he worked for a number of weeks in Galilee on an archaeological dig. Carmen spent several weeks in Hawaii helping a small church with its outreach program. She slept on a cot; she had no hot water or air-conditioning. Our son-in-love spent a week in a remote region in Argentina equipping pastors.

Family trips often provide a greater opportunity for learning than the school classroom. Current news articles come alive because the family has been or is going where the events described are happening. Our home is full of mementos from these years of travel. If you can't envision a Jewish *mezuzah*, check the doorposts at Magnolia Hill. If you are curious about how women grind their meal in Ethiopia, look at the doll in our garden room. If you have never held an animal-skin bottle, see one from the Beersheva bedouin market. If you have no concept of Africa, visit my husband's office and be surrounded by a host of mounted African animals.

Don't give your children the impression that there is nothing to be done in the United States. Involve yourselves as a family in helping the needy in your community. When our daughter Carmen's church committed to help some needy families at Christmas, granddaughter Abigail joined us on a shopping trip to select a winter coat for a needy child. When the son of one of our professors died of cancer, our son Armour made his way through a treacherous ice storm in the early morning hours to help the family make arrangements for transfer of the body and for the memorial service. At our church in Dallas, when an international student showed up with no place to live and no confirmed plans for his education, Armour and Carmen discovered his plight and suggested we take him home with us. He lived with us for a year and attended the Criswell College. Armour and Carmen taught him English, transported him to and from school, and helped him adjust to living in the States.

People come and go for many different reasons, but the welcome remains. In my old age, sometimes I long for solitude, but I don't think I'll ever lose my desire to have an open hearth to anyone God may send to my door.

Parents should never *assume* that their children will adopt their commitments in standards of speech, dress, and lifestyle. Their standards, which should be based on biblical principles, must be taught as well as caught! When I was a teenager, I will never forget my father's lessons concerning total abstinence from the use of alcoholic beverages. Daddy had an ambulance service as well as a mortuary; so he worked in the midst of suffering and death, of crisis and sorrow. One evening he returned home particularly crestfallen. He told me about a tragic accident in which a drunken driver had hit a car carrying some of my high school friends who had been attending a youth event at a nearby church. They were all killed, but the intoxicated driver walked away. Until now, I have never been tempted to take even a sip of alcoholic beverage.

Parents cannot be content to assume their children will adopt only habits and convictions emulated in their home. They must be proactive in setting a standard and making an "apology" or defense for the standard. Just saying no is not enough. Children and teens need to be given well-reasoned explanations for what you expect of them in daily living.

Parents should use God's Word to set standards for their children. For example, the Bible speaks clearly on the subject of sex. God created man and woman for a monogamous union, which means that He expects young people to remain virgins until after marriage and then to be faithful to their spouses for a lifetime.[7] The Bible also teaches that homosexuality is wrong.[8] In addition, a warning is given to avoid people or places where you might be tempted, and even drawn, to violate God's rules.[9] God expects the boundaries to be clear. Even physical touching becomes wrong when it ignites passion between a man and woman who have not been united by the covenant of marriage. For most, this leaves room for holding hands, hugging, and even kissing but not in empty houses or cars parked on deserted roads or uninhabited beaches.

Magnolia Hill was occupied by presidents first of Wake Forest University and then of Southeastern Baptist Theological Seminary. The stately English Tudor home sits on a small rise or hill of a beautiful estate lot highlighted by what once was the largest and most beautiful magnolia tree in our state. When I first drove up the steep drive, I named the home "Magnolia Hill." The name quickly caught on, and the spacious home has continued to be noted for its hospitality. Then came the hurricane and tornado, and our magnificent and majestic tree received what seemed a fatal blow. That blow, however, gave us a new view of the tree. An aged central trunk (planted in 1834) had spawned a host of smaller magnolias encircling its center. Growing upward, the boughs and branches knit together so that it appeared as one tree.

How like the family, who would have a center of strength (as the trunk of our historic magnolia) that is not seen by anyone else until disaster strikes. But once stricken the strength within radiates out and rallies to enable the unit to remain strong and become beautiful once more. Bright leaves, fragrant blooms, beautiful symmetry, stately dignity—all originated from the strong and vital trunk at its center. The outer embellishments caught the eye and awakened lingering admiration, but the true character of the tree—its genesis and strength—lay within the boughs hidden from public gaze.

Parents cannot depend on the church, religious school, or any parachurch organization to do spiritual nurture. They by all means should enlist help, but parents can take the responsibility to be sure that nothing is missing.

LEADING THE RIGHT WAY

Parents have the biggest stake in the well-being of their own children. They must assume primary responsibility for the important task of disciplining the child. Too often discipline is seen as being confined to prescribed punishment. However, in truth, discipline is the training of a child, molding his character, helping him learn to live in the world. *Training involves molding what is given, correcting what is wrong, strengthening what is right, and perfecting what is in process until the task is complete.* Someone has well said that the process of discipline is a program in which the parent makes a disciple out of his child! Underlying such a program is the necessity of spending time with your child, earning the child's respect and trust, and then modeling in your own life what you want to teach the child.

This third biblical principle for rearing children—leading them to go God's way via consistent discipline—may be the most challenging of all. It requires unconditional love, unending patience, relentless determination, consistent follow-through, and individualized creativity. The goal for parents is to lead their children to go God's way by equipping them with character qualities and virtues coming from the teachings found in the Bible. They must use a combination of lifestyle training and discipline in order to help children, by whatever persuasive means are required, to be obedient.

The book of Proverbs expresses parental responsibility in this way: "Train a child in the way he should go, And when he is old he will not turn from it."[10] "Train" (Heb. *chanak*) suggests "putting something into the mouth." The word referred to the Hebrew practice of opening the throat of a newborn.

The midwife, after delivering the baby, would dip her fingers into crushed dates and then massage the gums of the baby so that the sweet-taste on her fingers would stimulate sucking from the baby. This prelude prepared the way for the infant's taking and assimilating nourishment at his mother's breast. The same word was used to describe breaking a wild horse by means of a rope in his mouth. This message admonishes parents to be committed to channeling the will of a child to seek God's way instead of his own path. To fail in this task is to lay a foundation for self-willed living from which the child will not depart!

Many people are deceived in believing that the child must first be taught—given facts and information—which later would become the foundation for trained behavior. Actually the opposite is true. A child's training must begin long before formal teaching. Training begins at birth as a program of discipleship in which parents move a child through learning *parent-controlled* behavior to adopting *self-controlled* or independent behavior.

The goal is not to change the nature or personality of the child but rather to govern how he expresses his nature. In fact, for parents committed to the Judeo-Christian worldview, the final step is to move your child to a *God-controlled* lifestyle in which the child learns to make wise, God-honoring decisions. No longer is the child governed by his own willfulness and going his own way. Rather, he is committed to God's way.[11]

Some child-rearing experts suggest that a parent must break the child's *will*. To call for such action is to misunderstand the will. No one accomplishes anything without a will to do so. The will is the seat of choice and motivation. You cannot decide between two courses of action without using the will. At the heart of fulfilling every duty is the will to move forward with a particular task. To crush the will is to make the child a useless and thoughtless entity with no purpose in life. On the other hand, a parent does have the responsibility to break a child's determination to go *his own way* and miss God's best in life.

Selfish willfulness is a tragic path for the child. The Bible repeatedly warns against allowing a child "to go his own way" or seek "his own fancies."[12] My own understanding of the Proverbs 22:6 admonition to parents is clear in my personal translation or paraphrase from the Hebrew text: "Train up a child to go his own way, And when he is old he will not depart or abandon going his own way." A child who grows accustomed to having his own way may well show promise in the ability to make good choices early on—so much so that his parents are lulled into letting him consistently do as he pleases. The tragedy may be slow in coming, but come it will as he begins to make wrong choices with ease and confidence because he is convinced that his way is best.

The parent's task is never to be taken lightly as he must use every means at his disposal to set apart the child's will to holy and wholesome objectives. The parent cannot permit the child to do only what he wants to do. A battle naturally ensues between the will of the parent and the will of the child because genuine obedience demands cooperation of the will. The child must learn to do what he ought to do when he is told to do it whatever his personal feelings may be. This life lesson has ramifications that follow the child in all of life.

Consequences for disobedience must be clear, but before reaching this ultimate contest, a parent must lovingly and patiently guide the child into the right way, helping him to obey. This action takes a tremendous investment of time and energy.

Children learn to obey the commands of their parents, while they develop sensitivity to the guidelines presented to them by their parents. They are then under *parent-control.* The next step is *self-control,* a phase of development during which children reach the plateau of no longer needing continual parental supervision because their spirits and wills have been molded into such self-control and discipline that they make appropriate choices and decisions on their own. The process should not end with self-control; for ultimately a child should be prepared to order his life according to God's way and to govern his actions according to biblical principles. The child has then reached the highest plateau—*God-control.* There most certainly will be a battle en route to this goal, for the world is obsessed with the importance of making a child feel good about a self-centered focus. In fact, this ideology of elevating self-image or self-esteem above all else permeates everything a parent does. It elevates personal rights in the child and tears down personal discipline and self-control. It brings to the forefront achieving personal desires and goals in lieu of giving yourself in service to God and others.

One of the most challenging aspects of this lifestyle training is the control that must be present in the life of the one who is administering the training. A child will never respect what his parents have to say if they fail to emulate those teachings in their own lives. *To stand for what is right is one thing; to order your own life according to what is right is something else.*

Any inconsistency in the life pattern of parents will not only be noted but also will usually be magnified in the lives of their children. To fail to have their children live by the standards they present to others is devastating to those outside the family as well as to those within. Compromise, when embraced, can be a deadly weapon.

Parents do well to guard against inconsistency of life in their own lifestyle or example, in the discipline they expect of others as compared to the discipline they administer to their own children, and in their communication of biblical truth to others as the same they would communicate to their own children. Attending worship services, reading the Bible, praying, participating in family devotional time are all important. But if these are done perfunctorily without a genuine heart commitment, they are empty and meaningless to your children as well as to you.

The Bible is full of examples in which a parent's sin shows up in the life of his child: David, whose son Absolom tried to become king by killing his own father; Solomon, whose polygamy and pagan marriages made it impossible to produce godly seed for the throne and inevitable that the kingdom would be divided; Eli, whose personal commitment and position as a prophet and priest of Israel were not enough to prevent the deaths of his own sons in shame and ignominy before the Lord because of their spiritual disobedience. Eli appeared to honor his sons above God when he allowed them to sin openly without any effective effort to correct them.[13]

Many parents tend to shun their responsibilities with older children because the task seems impossible or because they fear losing their relationship with the child. Ignoring a child's sin is programming that child for disaster. If a child will not honor and obey his parents in earthly things, can a parent really expect the child to obey God in the heavenly sphere? But the tragedy of Eli reminds parents that their job of preparing the next generation has no retirement plan! Parents can't be concerned about what their children may think or say; they, too, must obey God. He expects parents to hold the standard high. True love will correct, reprove, and discipline. Parents ought to fear the Lord—not their kids!

There are some spiritual lessons to be learned. First, discipline is not primarily an assessment of penalty for wrong but is more an unveiling of God's care for His children. God spanks or chastises those whom He loves. He uses discipline to remind you that you are His child.[14] Parental discipline also prepares a child for obedience to God's authority.[15] Spiritual formation is the most important fruit from godly discipline.

The world's view of authority vacillates between anarchy and tyranny. God's pattern for authority is loving service and committed responsibility. A parent is wise to lead a child to submit to discipline and recognize it as molding life and character even if a child may despise it, chafe under it, or faint because of it.[16]

Parents should not pretend they have never made mistakes. If they make a mistake, they need to be accountable and seek forgiveness even from a child. A parent cannot fool his child. Whether or not you as a parent have a genuine commitment to the Lord, whether or not spiritual things are important to you, whatever really takes first place in your life will be evident to your children.[17] The problem in achieving discipline that moves the child toward God-control begins with the kind of training administered. *An inadequate kind of training, ineffective ways of doing the training, an insincere administrator of the training, and ineffectual examples for the trainees all contribute to inferior and incomplete training.*

Behavior that produces desirable results tends to recur, while behavior that brings undesirable consequences for the child is not as likely to happen again. Behavior that is not rewarded is far less likely to become ingrained and often completely disappears.

Unfortunately, many parents who show concern for the physical and social development of their children ignore their spiritual needs. They assume that regular attendance in church and participation in church youth activities, enrollment in a Christian school, coupled with prayer at mealtimes and sometimes even a form of family devotions will give their child the spiritual foundation necessary to have a productive life.

Parents dare not leave children to fend for themselves in the very dangerous world in which we live. There are certain benchmarks in a child's life that should be given special attention in parental training. For example, Dr. James Dobson suggests that parents take a preteen (eleven- or twelve-year-old) on a trip. Away from distractions, siblings, and peers, the child moving toward puberty is more likely to give attention to his parents. Parents, too, can give their undivided attention to sharing the moral values and biblical principles they have set in the foundations of their family heritage. Challenging topics like sex education and the natural physical changes that come with adolescence can be introduced and emphasized as needed. The get-away can also include some fun and laughter, inspiration and encouragement.

Parents must learn to hold their children close with supervision and interaction in all of life, but a day comes when they must let them go. If the foundation has been laid correctly, careful training in the early years will give children the confidence they need to move out of that supervision to their own reconnaissance and will give parents the peace to allow them to do that.

Dealing with strong-willed children requires godly wisdom and wise strategy. A strong-willed child is often willing to die for the right to do things his way. Much of your discipleship of such a child is by inspiring him to do the right thing.

In order to counteract the weaknesses found in a strong-willed child, consider these strategies:

- Make the child feel unique and special.
- Use "let's" or add "OK?" instead of direct orders.
- Choose your battles since you can't die on every hill.
- Never give up helping the child learn to obey, but lighten up heavy-handed communication.
- Reaffirm to the child that he is loved unconditionally.

You who are parents must pull and push and do whatever you have to do to get your children to go God's way. You move your children into their own decision-making process by holding them in a pattern of obedience to you. Children must never lose sight of the ultimate authority in their lives. They must move from *parent-controlled* to *self-controlled* to *God-controlled* behavior, and you as parents are responsible for not letting them loiter along the way!

1. Among the girls, the percentage rose from 80.2 percent in 1980 to 83.1 percent in 1995. For boys, it increased from 69.4 percent in 1980 to 72.9 percent in 1995. Cited in David Popenoe and Dafoe Whitehead, "The Vanishing Father," *Wilson Quarterly,* 20, no. 2 (1996): 19–21.

2. Maggie Gallagher, "Marriage-Saving," *National Review,* 8 November 1999, 38–40.

3. 2 Tim. 1:5.

4. 2 Tim. 3:15.

5. Deut. 6:4–6.

6. Deut. 6:6–9.

7. Gen. 2:24.

8. Rom. 1:24–28.

9. 1 Cor. 6:18.

10. Prov. 22:6.

11. Heb. 12:10–11.

12. Prov. 1:28–31; 3:5–7.

13. 1 Sam. 2:29.

14. Heb. 12:7–8.

15. Heb. 12:9–10.

16. Heb. 12:11–13.

17. Prov. 23:26.

9

Is There Any Help for the Family?

ALTHOUGH THE "VILLAGE" OR COMMUNITY has a role, it must not overpower, ignore, or undermine the family. Communities can return the strength of the family by banding together to recover family time from the overscheduled hyperactivity and consumer culture that plagues society. For example, competitive sports have evolved into year-round cycles, and parents are pushed from standing on the sidelines to sitting in the upper tiers of the grandstand. They furnish money for uniforms and equipment and an audience for the event, but they give up family dinners, worship, traditions, reunions, and even vacations to plan all of life around a child's athletic competitions. Athletic competition is not bad in itself; but if it becomes the be-all and end-all of life, it loses its value and destroys much more.

Instead of abdicating control of family time to the school, business, community, sports, and even synagogues and churches—however well-meaning these may be—a family can become proactive in developing the "solitary" within its own circle. Parents must become intentional about protecting family time by setting limits. Kids may whine; coaches may rant and rave; schools may threaten or cajole; but family time should be the precious treasure on a pedestal! Extracurricular activities do have a place, but they must be kept in balance with the whole of life.

NEIGHBORS AND FRIENDS

A neighborhood may be full of families who strive to work together and watch out for the kids within its community. However, the first and most effective line of defense for protecting children has been and always will be the family. Institutions coming out of and being put together from families should not superimpose themselves over families.

A *crisis of character* has quickly become a *crisis in culture.* People are beginning to realize that the family is in trouble with repercussions in every area of life. When the family is sick, religious institutions, government, community, and schools better begin taking aspirin!

THE CHURCH OR SYNAGOGUE

A new study confirms that people who go to a synagogue or church regularly tend to have lower blood pressure, stronger immune systems, and lower rates of cancer, heart disease, and mental illness. As a result, they live longer.[1] When people stop believing in God, the danger is not so much in believing nothing as it is in believing anything. A belief system is not absent since in truth everyone believes in something.

The standard has been removed, and standard-bearers have been portrayed as misfits and radicals. Role models and heroes have been replaced by standard-breakers. Immorality has been elevated to new heights. It is explained away, excused, and even praised. Sports "heroes" are involved in grievous immorality in a public way, yet these men are still honored and admired.

Parents dare not abdicate their role in supervising the spiritual nurturing of their children. When my son was in our church youth division, he came home one Sunday evening to report on a guest speaker who had blatantly stated that homosexuality was merely a genetic condition and thus a right lifestyle for some. The speaker avowed that he was homosexual but claimed that he was not sinning because he did not "practice" homosexual acts. The next Sunday evening I sat in the youth group to field some questions to the speaker. I sensed confusion and even annoyance among the leaders of the group. The following week my husband canceled his preaching engagement, and he was present for the youth meeting! The biblical teaching on homosexuality was clearly and unapologetically presented. Then each young person had a choice between two diametrically opposite views. Paige and I have always taken seriously our responsibility as parents to oversee the spiritual training of our children—even within the walls of an evangelical church.

THE NATION

The Roman state never forgot that the family was the footing of all civil social order. The state sought to safeguard and uphold the family. However, the impetus to commit oneself to the family and renew efforts to build a wholesome lifestyle around those family commitments will never be done through an executive order or an act of congress or a court ruling. Motives for such commitment must ultimately come from deep within the human heart, and those motives find deepest root within the family.

Government on every level needs to consider whether their programs and policies encourage effective parenting. Politicians should support parents rather than replace them. No legislation should be passed without considering its impact on families. Family-friendly government pays dividends. It provides a better quality of life and reduces social costs for government. Government welfare is a poor substitute for family responsibility.

No man-made institution can equal the God-made family when it comes to reinforcing the basic values of society. If government would spend its budget alleviating the economic stresses that have crept into the tax structure to oppress parents who are bearing and rearing children, the families who experienced relief from oppressive policies could then give their attention to do what government has proven it cannot do—prepare children for taking their places in society. Children who have effective parenting are much better equipped to become productive citizens.

The relevance of marriage to issues like crime, welfare dependence, joblessness, educational failure and drug addiction is clearly on record. The loosening of the divorce laws to make the dissolution of a marriage without consequences has now been statistically shown to parallel the startling rise in family breakup that began almost three decades ago. The no-fault divorce has been a factor in causing the number of divorces to soar.

WHAT GOOD FAMILIES ARE DOING RIGHT

Strong families have established the solitary in families through rituals and traditions that belong to them.

A strong and vibrant family will indeed adapt for its members certain ways of doing things or the doing of certain things. These rituals and traditions are markers to set them apart from others.

Good families are easy to recognize. Their strength seems to catapult them to a place of honor from which they can make a difference. These families are not perfect. They aren't made up of perfect people, nor do they have perfect circumstances in which to operate. Quite the contrary, some of the strongest and most exemplary families are functioning in the midst of tremendous adversities and trials. These families don't always agree, but they have learned to discuss their differences without hostility and to look for ways to bring their minds and hearts together. Even agreeing to disagree is done in a respectful and loving way.

Mothers and fathers model a living example of a strong and loving relationship with each other.

When husbands and wives model a happy and productive marital union, children are secure and happy. They can relax in the security their love for each other provides, and they can see in real life how a man and woman are to relate to each other in an exclusive monogamous relationship.

Parents are to pattern a disciplined lifestyle and control the environment in which their children are living.

Increasingly it is hard to protect your children and home from the invasion of ideas that are contrary to Christian principles and sound morality. Many bad influences on the home can easily be eliminated or controlled by hands-on parenting.

Character is formed and strengthened by resistance to evil, not by immunity to it and by wisdom to avoid wrong choices, not by insulation against harmful influences. The entertainment industry in general and television in particular have been identified as having a greater influence on children than anything else *except* maybe their parents. Families addicted to television lose interest in one another as they are mesmerized in front of the set. If properly monitored and kept in perspective, the television can be a tremendous device for initiating discussion on subjects of importance. Television programming should not become the backdrop for mealtime, the filler for all idle time, the entertaining baby-sitter for a bored child, the vehicle for learning and enrichment activities, or the exclusive window to the world (current events as well as classic literature).

A loving family majors in communication. They will listen to one another and respond with genuine sensitivity.

Most people are so busy thinking how they will respond or interject their own ideas into a conversation that they do not really listen to anyone else. The inability to listen is the most difficult problem of communicating within families. Family members are usually quicker to react than to respond. Reactions tend to reflect your own experiences and feelings, whereas responses are more likely to reflect the feelings of others. Especially is this true with busy parents who continue whatever they are doing, while going through the motions of listening to a child who may be hurting or rejoicing. The child needs to feel a rapport with and interest from the parent to whom he is speaking.

To listen haphazardly often means a premature and inappropriate response—i.e., reactionary or angry—instead of a carefully formulated and calmly delivered answer. Rather than taking time to stand in the shoes of the child, the parent may fire back with his own feelings and experiences with no attempt to get the child to share his own fears and feelings of inadequacy. A child, just like an adult, needs someone to hear about his fears and to feel his pain. Then there is time to move toward suggested solutions.

No time is better spent by a parent than hours just listening—when your child comes in from school, when a teenager returns from an outing with friends, when a young adult voices frustrations from the job, when a young mother shares the mundane daily events of your grandchild. When someone is intently listening to you, blocking out all other distractions, she is interested in you alone! And that makes you feel special!

Observing body language is also important. Family members need to learn to recognize unspoken messages. Understanding nonverbal messages is much more challenging than listening to words spoken. Only in the most intimate relationships do you care enough to observe the details in nonverbal communication—the eyes, the gestures, the general body language.

Parents communicate their own personal intimacy with one another through these nonverbal expressions—adoring glances at one another, gentle touches when passing, settling next to one another, a quick kiss. Touch is also one of the most effective ways to express love for a child—a telling smile, a thumbs up, a pat on the shoulder, a quick hug. Sometimes families have their own private set of signals to express their feelings to one another even in the midst of a crowd.

Nonverbal communication takes time and disciplined observation, but it adds a dimension to intimacy. All healthy families should strive for this careful reading of one another. The investment of time and energy is worth the effort.

In a healthy family people are expected to speak out with spontaneity. Polite propriety goes out the window! Sometimes even to finish a sentence is a challenge since nobody feels constrained to hold back. A sense of playfulness and a big dose of humor, together with some mischievous fun, appear during most family meals. Yet there should also be a balance of interaction among the family members.

A family has fun! They affirm and encourage one another.

Home is to be the center of relaxation, the place to which you run when you are discouraged or hurting. How better to relieve the tension and heal the hurts than by doing fun things as a family.

Parents have the responsibility to know their children. Two siblings can be amazingly different—even when they have come from the same womb and been reared in the same setting. These differences in personality and giftedness must be affirmed as family character traits are molded. Strong differences of opinion must be respected. Parents and children can disagree without being disagreeable.

Children have the opportunity to learn to articulate their beliefs and opinions in an atmosphere of loving respect. Teens are often not fettered with logic or reality, but they must be heard. Having an audience before whom they can argue their cases can also teach them to be accountable for their opinions, to defend their beliefs with sound reasoning, and to be willing to change a position when it is proven wrong. Winning or losing an argument is not success or failure in itself; rather, debate is a vehicle for more complete expression of what you believe and a means for verifying whether or not your position will stand in the marketplace of ideas. This intellectual sparring is also an arena for learning how to function in the real world.

The men in our family are into "Word of the Day" calendars with one-upmanship in process as each tries to work into the conversation his erudite word. Theological debate and political discussion are also common. Opinions differ; ideas are sometimes poles apart; emotions can be intense; but everyone has a turn at bat in the arena of family discussion.

The family demands respect for each member of the household.

Respect is a permeating influence in a healthy household. Demeaning words and/or put-downs have no place. Family members should give one another private space even in tight quarters. Parents should allow children some domain of privacy—if not a private room, a personal drawer or closet or box. This set-aside space should not be invaded unless there is strong evidence that the child is in danger physically, mentally, or emotionally.

Families must seek a way for reconciliation. They are to learn to "fight" fair, and peace ought always to be the goal. Disagreements are a part of healthy relationships. Effective ways to get an issue on the table must be found so that each person can present his case.

One of the first rules to consider is timing. Divisive and emotional issues have no place at the family mealtime for obvious reasons, nor should a fight be declared just as someone is leaving the house for an appointment or at bedtime. A timely discussion may diffuse an untimely explosion.

Opportunity must be given to allow for ample discussion of a matter that divides. Once subjected to extensive, rational discussion, the issue is to be resolved. If children cannot do this on their own, then a parent must become the peacemaker. Once solved, the issue is to be put aside and not continually dragged forth for use in future debate.

Our children had their "wars," especially during the teen years. They had an uncanny way of bringing out the worst in each other. My husband and I never doubted that they loved each other, but sometimes we weren't sure they liked each other! We worked on each of them to move toward peaceful and happy coexistence. One incident signaled real progress in reconciliation. When Carmen's senior class was at Nimrod's Castle in Israel, a steep path had to be maneuvered to the top. As I ascended, I turned to see Armour making his way up a bit slower than usual because he had Carmen on his back! Any brother who would carry a teenaged sister up such a challenging ascent on a hot summer day in the desert must think she is mighty special!

A family provides the atmosphere for children to learn respect for the opinions of others. Parents help their children learn how to fight fairly by doing so themselves. While parents are wise to do most of their heated arguments and any discussions concerning handling their children in private, there is a place for public difference of opinion so that children can observe how their parents handle these situations.

The family shares responsibility. Children must be taught to serve others.

Every member of the family should contribute to maintaining the well-being of the household. Chores must be assigned. Daily tasks should not always merit monetary compensation, though the family resources must also be shared. Learning that a workman is worthy of his hire is also a lesson to be taught.[2]

When our children entered high school, we worked out a comprehensive budget (everything except car and health insurance) to be divided into monthly or weekly installments, according to the child's preference. We wanted the children to learn the value of a dollar and the discipline of wisely spending and saving their money. They had to purchase their clothing, toiletries, school supplies, as well as any meals they elected to eat on their own. Of course, they also were expected to tithe their income.

A balance of interaction must be developed among family members. Though each family member will have assigned tasks, teamwork is also an easily cast vision. Children should be challenged to share the load of their parents.

When Paige and I were writing notes, compiling materials, and editing the Criswell Study Bible, we did not have word processing. We had to painstakingly cut, paste, and photo-copy in an effort to keep errors from entering the manuscript through ordinary retyping. Armour and Carmen sweetly, of their own volition, spent hours helping us.

Families should have a shared religious faith. Parents must teach their children virtues arising out of the common Judeo-Christian ethic.

The National Institute for Healthcare Research in Rockville, Maryland, gathers data on the impact of religion on health. The Institute cited research from the American Psychological Association indicating that couples who participated in reli-gious activities together had a higher level of marital satisfac-tion. It also reported that couples were more likely to solve their problems constructively.[3]

Family-friendly communities are important. Parents want to rear their children where concerned neighbors, active commu-nity groups, and vibrant churches and synagogues will be the backdrop for safe streets, strong schools, sound economies, and thriving towns and cities. Families shape their communities.

CONCLUSION

Family pride can be developed in a myriad of ways. But before it can take root, the family needs to determine what values its members will embrace. The Bible calls for the father to be the family leader, the mother his helper and the resident manager of the household, and the children to honor both parents with respect and obedience. Each member of the household is important and should know that he is accepted, loved, and trusted. Every family member is definitely part of the "in group"!

Achieving such is no small matter. Parents can plant seeds with music lessons, hobbies, and good books. Children can honor their parents and hear instruction from father and mother. Family members can learn to laugh at one another and determine to forgive one another. Instead of charging your home with tension and hostility, you can ventilate your dwelling with a relaxed environment and positive comments. Bitterness and grudges can be treated as worthless debris. Who you *are* can become far more important than what you *say.*

Creating a positive atmosphere with the free exchange of ideas within and the welcome mat without for family friends and even strangers will make your home magnetic to all who approach its door. At the same time togetherness should not be forced. Each member of the family needs some time away, especially times of solitude to develop a personal relationship with God. Each member of the family must presumably look within to find that "solitary" in the family—the bond that holds all together.

Home is a special concept. I can never seem to unload all the freight when trying to explain what home means to me. There is indeed a sweetness and fragrance associated with it as with no other—except perhaps *mother!* No matter how humble, home should be a sanctuary where you can live and learn to love your earthly family and a retreat where you can learn how to live for and love your heavenly Father.

Home should be a place of trust and security, a place where all members can feel at ease and speak freely and yet where there is ample love and kindness even in conflict. Home must be a place of ultimate intimacy in which there is respect for one another set in the midst of genuine joy that is unaffected by circumstances. Yes, home is designed to be an oasis in the desert of a cruel world. Home is the metaphor God chose to describe His own eternal abode, and every earthly home ought to be the family's "heaven on earth."

1. Analysis of forty-two peer-reviewed studies of 126,000 people conducted by the National Institute for Healthcare Research, Rockville, MD and published in *Bottom Line,* 15 August 2000.

2. 1 Tim. 5:18.

3. National Institute for Healthcare Research, Rockville, MD, in *Bottom Line,* 15 August 2000.

Conclusion

THE HOUSE WHERE YOU LIVE protects you from rain, heat, cold, snow, even storms. Your possessions, too, are kept safe. You can return to a secure place each day. You can eat, rest, and even cleanse yourself there. A home is much more. It provides boundaries and consistencies for molding character. It becomes a sanctuary in which you find physical rest and spiritual peace.

Children have passed from the control of their own parents to governance by community experts who are viewed as better equipped to train the next generation. This change in paradigm has replaced group living and being other-person oriented with a preference for individualism and being alone. Marriage with covenant and commitment has been overshadowed by cohabitation and bearing children outside of wedlock.

Destructive public policies have played a part in such drastic changes. The federal welfare policies make bearing children outside of marriage economically feasible. Illegitimate births have been subsidized, while families with children have borne the burden of taxation. If a mother chooses to remain in the home or if a couple marries instead of cohabiting, their taxes are higher. Government has succeeded in stripping both married couples and children of their economic value. Yet God has not left us without a pattern for the family. He gives simple yet profound principles. Some seem contrary to human instincts; all are paradoxical to the ways of the world.

During a visit to northern Wales, my husband and I noticed an estate home known for its beautiful gardens. I remain fascinated by Bodysgallen—"house among the thistles." Home should be just that! In a world of thorns and prickly foliage that inflict pain and suffering, your home should be a haven and refuge, a beautiful garden to which you can retreat for rest and relaxation and safety.

God calls for a husband and wife in marriage to leave their birth families and past loyalties and to cling in faithful commitment to each other. He describes such a union as "one flesh," a whole new entity fashioned from the supernatural gluing of two parts so that they become one.[1] The husband in this union is to love his wife selflessly—to provide for her, to protect her, and to lead her.[2] The wife is to submit herself in gracious cooperation as a complementary helper.[3] If God gives the opportunity for parenthood, father and mother are to nurture their children in the Lord.[4] Children are to respond with honor for and obedience to their parents.[5]

A family committed to following biblical patterns will enjoy true intimacy. Husband and wife are united in their purposes and goals.[6] Their unity is not only in body through physical intimacy but also in oneness of mind, heart, spirit, and soul.

Husband and wife also have the opportunity to link hands with God Himself to create another life. From their love may come a child who is both the fruit of their love and the unique blending of themselves. With mother and father, children can find safety, nurture, and loving care. They learn the lessons of life not merely from words but from lives modeled before them. In the home, children learn about God. Spiritual formation takes place. Character, strength, and stability move them toward adulthood and independent living.

The home is a place of worship where children learn spiritual truths; there faith is found and fortified. A child learns basic wisdom and becomes acquainted with the world and its vast knowledge. The home is also a child's first touch with governance and law and order as he is taught to conform to what is right and where he is punished for disobedience.

The family is also a living metaphor chosen by God to reveal Himself to the people of the world. God speaks of Himself as *Father* and of His creation as *children,* and He refers to the afterlife abode He has prepared as a heavenly home. His unconditional love and lovingkindness are to be modeled, though inadequately, in the human family.

Halekulani, a Hawaiian word meaning "house befitting heaven," is the name of an award-winning Waikiki Beach property. The hotel offers its guests "seclusion without isolation," and your home should offer an oasis of tranquility, attentive service, caring nurture, and unconditional love in the heart of a tumultuous world. You should indeed have the serenity of solitude in the midst of loyal love.

What is the home? Is it a residential hotel with maid service, a fast-food restaurant where the food is free, or just a place to store your belongings? I believe home is family. Family members live, learn, and grow together. Home provides security—a haven or retreat from the problems of the world. It should be marked with love and acceptance and laced with fun and fellowship. The home is not a human invention or a cultural phenomenon; it is God's idea from start to finish.

Can families have happy endings? The author of Ecclesiastes wrote, "Better is the end of a thing than its beginning."[7] Through faith in God's providence and commitment to doing things His way, you can indeed move down a path to ultimate happiness and joy. Families are the earthly vessel through which a mother and father and their children can bind themselves together in loving devotion and face whatever may come with the confidence that with one another and the Lord they can indeed overcome the obstacles of life and find happiness. That outward happiness is not dependent upon people or circumstances but comes from inner strength and an internal bubbling spring of joy.

1. Gen. 2:24; Eph. 5:31.
2. Gen. 2:15–17; Eph. 5:25–29.
3. Gen. 2:18; Eph. 5:21–24; 1 Pet. 3:1–6.
4. Ps. 127; Eph. 6:4.
5. Exod. 20:12; Eph. 6:1–3.
6. Ps. 34:3.
7. Eccl. 7:8.